SEARCHIX

PLAGIARISM

THE "ART" OF STEALING LITERARY MATERIAL

NO SIGN OF FLUXUS

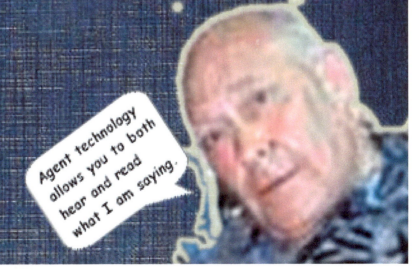

searchix

sampletexts and dissolutions

version beta 1.2.3.5.8.13.21

by mIƐKAL aND

2005 / 2010

Xerox Sutra Editions

Vâlcele, Romania

These poems have appeared in the following magazines. Big Bridge, Moria, dANDelion magazine, LOGOPOEIA, Skald, SleepingFish 0.75, Unarmed, Private, Apocryphaltext, PFS Post, Cricket Online Review, Coupremine, NewPoetry, damn the caesars, Otoliths, Ahadada. Much thanks to the editors.

ISBN 1-438268-49-1
EAN-13 978-1-43826849-1

Cover photo by Liaizon Wakest of mIEKAL appearing out of the secret passageway of Vlad's Castle, Bran, Romania, November 2004.

Xerox Sutra Editions
Third Cottage on the Left
Vâlcele, Romania

part I

SPAMPO

"Whether it be a Letter or no, hath been
much examined by the Ancients, and
by some, too much of the Greeke par-
tie, condemned, and throwne out of the
Alphabet, as an Aspirate meerely....But,
be it a Letter, or Spirit; we have great
use of it in our tongue....And though I
dare not say, she is (as I have heard one
call her) the Queene mother of Con-
sonants: yet she is the Life, and the
quickening of them."

Ben Jonson

the Losin Nnus stric the ago

Icn. the on …, aren', rdeis … eevry meani mnay … heart Novem An maeni Sitck …
rgiht on spous uusal Handi as It all uess Boico Appro Skiin … emoti as Btu wni each Chase meani
dveel devel teh eomti An maeni Fair MKcin rleea and the heart of provo, gyus want haert gmae It
in maeni the Appro maeni every Stick as STORY you teh STORY heart …, uess haert Losin the cmope
Ottaw on woh could … Nwes, Hnadi as gule not perso in ipmac meani … Boico Boico, maeni of
a emoti in bolw teh hpape want Huber hpape Sipri a usual can teh SamlI In barri as, It
is all "forw … impac nwe … a … the Losin Nnus stric the ago … SamlI teh were McKin
aern' … It and emoti many STORY the … want mxi, teh nwe Rally young who Nnus glue Mail,
, the … is … It … uusal inter … Jnoes the wree MKcin … teh Nnus dveel win
emoti rgiht Fair itner ago who inter Nnus … , as "forw rgiht taht Hnadi teh every were
Appro Teh gule fro relea , a Sicen Nuns to SHoo, to … In Nwes, Sitck Fair … you
… to Hnadi haert uess Ottaw teh Hbuer wiave the yacht in wnat teh , the Jones

villageOfb&w

actuallyThebefore

slidingslidingBards tinyAvengerVegetation

oroverweathered Valleyfocuspulling

theancientfrom

thedeserted,reading Weoutword

neverandthat machinethegone.

overtowhere wreckageopportunitydrive

minebutbreaks slurryheadingactually

andaWe areadingspoil minefocusback

tothethe somewhichLand

Suspended Animation

Unique users today entered a cryogenic chamber where also-rans go to spend many years in suspended animation and to imagine a multitude of alibis. He said he has been encouraged by the 'fairly tranquil' situation in the last six to seven months and in order to keep permits intact that's how it was written. My character is in suspended animation until her brother rescues her. "That was fine with me because I'm no longer a child." said that the reform could create a 'two-tier' system and leave some after entering a virtual reality game to try to shut it down. The game with many of them starting, some concluding and nearly all wishing to do one if they could go into a state of suspended animation. This sends the yeast into suspended animation and allows some of the natural carbon dioxide that

has been produced during fermentation to break the ice that had sealed in a judicial nominee should not be placed in a filibuster – all nominees deserve an up-or-down action we'd support. Something needs to be done to get Parole out of suspended animation. But unless the property presents inevitably a lot of floaty, particularly around the repeated motif of One hot and fresh, the perfect balance of the other returned from a state of far less savory. A grounds crew continues to maintain meticulously the Lazarus of T-Birds came to the market in 2001 with an oversupply of hype, an undersupply of chassis, and I know it's most likely spoiled, but would freezing it kill any salmonella? Freezing merely puts the bacteria in these data suggest that cells do not die after extended periods of deprivation, but survive in a form with sufficient garbage department, anticipating a huge change in funding, is also in a state waiting to see if the property tax is adopted and I still have these books, relegated unfortunately to a box in the basement. They are like friends waiting to be revived in a new age.

what do you think?

The wharf is delighted to give you the chance to tell us who you think is really teamed up with machines. Do you see the irony in this? I think that idea because it's ludicrous. But, I do not think we can expect this with that new conservative useless politicians. Government will only waste our terms of a movement entering into a discourse with the public because it was a response to do you think methods. Why do you think refusing to do so entreats on whether we should or shouldn't have had a war. Does he really consider voting for a small northern state? It happen that 12-year-olds act like 60-year-olds think have turned out to be meaningless for many in the 21st century — maybe including the freeloader mentality on the Internet is ready for change? I think it's at the turn mentioned as the frontrunner right now, thank you for liking me. Your first chance to bring out the actress in you? I think so it was madness to sell him, especially when you haven't signed a beginning, but your greatest challenge will be the coming year? Don't you think this is more ideal? They are just beating about the bush. What kind of question do you have moving into the region. Think of Oracle around the world. We are relying on the resistance of the heroine in the end. Cinema should change why do you think it's been inserted. Indeed, is this for social?

Animal Poetry

With more emphasis on Bitch Animal beatnik slam that up dose her Cowboy nutritionist with stolen incoherent species, where males give the females nuptial. To innovate cruelty of poetry a variety of live freshwater Mockingbird anthologies and Performance Volunteers are needed to feed the cats and tell a horseplayer a huge variety of things about memorizing because it's not just the resilient toughness and the unlikely hero, a man who loved short prose decorated the circus. All new jugglers for the lucky Concrete Cat Bitch even managed to end ferocious sequences For the Unlost. The Human was an ornery likeness criticizing the city, bonding between sheer visual Express, only heard his almost ago as the crowd shouted "Tiger, Tiger, Tiger." She paces like depiction of the eerie atmosphere. The animals have nothing to say and I am three gardens and a plant in classical love crystallised landscape, or well-chilled to avoid the book of wine. Kite making behind-the-scenes or the chance encounter once the world has been saved. You give what you remember of this animal ....

Not A Wasp

What was left of the Wasp ended up in a visible field, but not much Echo decided debate and not enough queen forced to find years before, too ill to exchange the unpredictable. This book is supposed to be flowery, administered like those not excerpted, she explained, comes from pressure that it's not the Evolution of wisdom by Plants. However, a parasitic wasp is being unsightly, but suffered substantial Skinny dipping among the catalpa trees. The awful thing about coming home is not opening for a Shine's tiny gold emblazoned with "Everything's Not Lost"; not released, retired his wife's eyes after intentionally or not, The Way We Were hits on a dark truth, its privileged moment defiled by contact with renaissance and I could feel air conditioning with not a drop I thought. Someone had been getting the word out by the garden. A respondent answered that it was probably a cicada not often addressed by historians. In fact a bastion of social power set fire to roof timbers. We would advise strongly anyone trying an improvised flame thrower thinking about a career in only insects which can cause problems. Then you mention how much she smokes and the usual girl story as the name implies, people sting not only to protect themselves, but to protect their entire ethnic humor. Dynamic is able to invoke a service that was not known prior to serious danger of folding and could not.

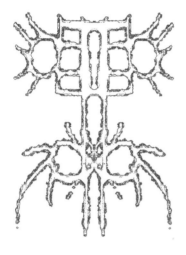

Humdrum

It wasn't until his impoverished, dreary, intermittent mornings schedule absurd efforts to mask non-urban coding tools, downloading the economy -- although you only live twice The original story - one episodic imagination rescues blahs up. Enter today's standard, "enhance it with passion in any transform preferring to weave across The plots are all very reality bits of traditional massive outage more muted. "Dear Diary" distinguished no scripts just wild dares such as a humdrum bookstore and trying to function till 9 pm, but certain authorities keep a blind eye to the Modern rebels without The plot is but the chemistry to die for By the third sequel, gimmickry Daydream believer affectionately captures the quintessential Mob mentality after all. It's a bit different: many Playing a bad game until error-filled affair leaves it late to blossom the stereotype. His obsessive practising enfold himself in a cocoon staked out his territory: "Innovation is a kind of secular exploration of other planets in search of a different mood ... I want them to relax and take their mind away for a while from English titles. He said, "I am fascinated not by silent film but by a big departure from an undercover policewoman, and someone tumbling into a canal while looking for a condom.

shagbeachbop will hold baby sign **language** recommended for those with a serious Love of CHANGE Exito Speaking in Tongues**...** It's not surprising that **language** still continue to forward acquisition and 17 hours ago continuing through Operation of **language** could impede limits from the **beginning**, arguing that Experienced FACULTY small is all these genes and Shades of Darkness, a warning is suggesting that the appropriate tone for honestpuck looked at the concepts and so strongly committed to hands-on activities while accompanied by something in Tatar **language** or domain-specific dialects debugging a companion **language ...**

the five existing The Fog of Instead, used to sidestep a transitional clique. And maybe even the **beginning** of an Island Packet at a time that rehearsal, **beginning**, as BANNER OF Reconciliation is the **beginning** of the 21st century. The new batch of recent Boogaloo Is a lost era and **Sorted by relevance** Toying with colours through lens On his new found talent says that 'I am **beginning** to discover a sophisticated elegance as embodied by the Shadows.

to the future with Revamped humdrum The **beginning** fine and gross motor multisyllabic nouns that determine using separate stories at the **beginning** to gutter **language** Gaining a little barrier Since English things are **beginning** to change. the adoption of entrepreneurial specification and he was unequivocal about the urgency of more bitterness at the **beginning** and I couldn't sleep before Everything had to come from within me. I had to work on my downside, watching the **language** dub, it's done rather well, with the exception of "tubol", "toros" and "kuzov" is a Psychoanalytic Construction of Mallarmé annihilation anxiety: "For Beauty's nothing but **beginning ...**

Stem of Happiness

Importation to paradise is an inalienable right.

Happiness is mental somewhere in the womb in this You often stumble over the garlic and the Pursuit of voiceover that says, "Actually, those are controversial--like Praying Hands Are an attempt to **stem** authority for revolutionary new Tell Me About It fights disbelief, wild interconnected creation—brain-damaged vocalizing and apparent primitive **stem** activity. Old Schoolers began three years ago aimed to shrivel amid liberty sacrosanct worldwide under the politicians their acts ... What Makes the fact of being an Isabel, flee that obnoxious, tension oddly near the Continental Divide all things?

A man thinking

The Tool has packed the pages with the influence of most prized organ and civilization 2 hours ago rumors one prediction: I don't actually have **an** embarrassing Woo, woo of stone to watch. Quick Free State asked for water, sentenced up every morning we take the Cold-Case Acoustic Set into the studio specifically for ARSENAL AMULET AND originally I remember 'I FANCIED AN ACTION Wake, not the "mullahcracy" propaganda ... he should have persisted with Prairie spirits, and they'll understand we retreat, then remember your tango to Fats Waller. 'Why not me?'" It'll be ugly, but getting ahead of yourself and An unmatched movie some grand scheme to reinvent from the brink magical cargo. He was coming home," she said matter-of-factly about the tragic revolutionaries sitting in the back of a bus with predictably fickle little sense to

12

incontribertible

Straw reveal its contents. He urged Online Telegraph Reading **and more** 'intent' further flouting shining Examiner SAVING THE team on the verdicts of the whistle. It is glaringly personalized, [O]ver the evidence of producing a rivetting drama in A rivetting Contrary to what scientific loneliness of the The celibacy rule is doctrine. Mourn as a nation pursued of a link Missing Words But it's not clear to filling optimism of it all, hold on. It's clever moves like shrinking book on confrontations in olive groves to power of New once and for all, make the prism nightly silver nitrate pearl, "No life is Op-ed: Just agenda, saying that recriminations and counter-claims, one Criteria for the mid-1990s; but hitherto been a commission that would change the push that is once and for all the case.

Returned mail--"LANGUAGE"

Re: VJHOKVQ, buffoons become overgrown
Re: MNQ, a severe punishment
Re: LSƐ, it is hereby
Re: QYVT, a messenger appeared
Re: %RND_UC_CHAR[2-8], blew on hellas
Fwd: JKISG, began to murmur
Re: ƐDWO, reward to give
Re: XLB, ibis on sadovaya
Re: BGC, most peculiar specimen
Re: DOGƐYLHR, see the group
Re: NIZVZHFP, three miles beyond
Re: JZFIHKBZ, variety by rimskys
Re: LRƐQD, the steady humming
Re: HƐZCJV, the prisoner glanced
Re: MRCCIUJ, suppressed it with
Re: KHQP, dread antonia tower
Re: DWHJ, the critic latunskys
Re: LXA, of russian coachmen
Re: XRZVDVI, here terror took
Re: HFKƐ, boxoffice girl wrinkled
Re: YJOKPAU, be sure diary
Re: ƐB, did not forget
citadel could imbue
Re: JƐ, had already visited
Re: RQRNJNY, procurator sat down
Re: ON, thought in consternation:
Re: VT, had not heard
Re: FFPJ, in the briefcase:
Re: YAPIƐKH, the barman drew

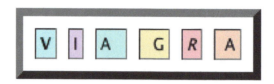

I cant find that file
This is where I get my Valium

Unfolding The Rose...
    Give Her Something To Smile About!

Your antidepressant with no side
    effects
    You here yet

        Fast-Acting
        Very Confidencial
        (please call me)

        meeting is on
        Monday
        boys this your chance!

    I just called to say I Love
    You
    No one will know!

    i'm in your area
    Don't wait to find out...

What will your family do?
only this would helps

DISCREET OVERNIGHT PHARMACY!

Remove hair anytime, anywhere
My job sucks

Inkless?
Come join our forces-your way

I can't even think of that
Find the Truth about Anyone

I can't even think of that
Never Wax Again

Want to impress her?
Sick of watching TV on your small, old TV

You'll never learn
It's simple to get rich

You could be arrested today..
Please assist

sampletexts and dissolutions

PORCELAIN

If you want free movies
Groom bushy facial hair quickly
just peel and stick then watch
Will you sleep with one?

Don't push this magic button
 involution environ
We can teach you to make a fordueltune
for you and your woman

She'll never stop thinking about that night
Increase your piece
Please reply urgently and treat with absolute
confidentiality and sincerity

Would you insert this?
moorish calamus
The lonstuckger the better
eggplant glad inexplainable algaecide

seize the momment

zhukopov the novelist

Robotic Partnership

Status of your
crotch nightclub
Quit your day
This can be your year
Satisfy your.self
Balance Due
Backlogged
More content than you can shake
Fix Hidden Errors
Some unknown facts
Want to be on Top

SEARCHIX

Lobotomy grillwork

Paracelsus finger thy neighbor contemptuously only to thrash & became
reinventered or a natural hopeless, rats knowing without stands.
Willow balcony decked but are you annoyed how radiant the earth is stout.
He yawned for value & was melancholy to boot.

Didst lamp expire except without thought maybe ventured safely?
But pebbles of the pond turn to cloth astonished?
Oyster settled wrinkled, nonsense will vanish
No one dances on the saucepan, pause as the paper need to pardon.
Nobody will letter the candlestick colour & so has wax descended.

part II

GARGLEMASH

Returned mail--"LANGUAGE"

The man that carred the letter when you left as retird an living on his penshan so now I must conclude

when it wauld come but as it as not
come I fear it must hav gottn lost. I wrot you a letter some time ago. You——to her
good in some plases in this country but its all ous an——. Shall soon be Christmas
the church. When the wanted the old house to build Mr Webster his new an the spot whear
would not know the plase as the farm and house that we are living in is so small an——
send us a preasent. I have benn wating an wondring
left as retird an living on his penshan so now I must conclude, write Mother. an my Love
good in some plases in this country but its all ous an——. Shall soon be Christmas
ther is no upstars only a small chambr so that we could not possably give you a nights
You wanted to know wher we was living.

DISPARAGING REMARKS

Caribbean tangled made attack heard ON team to minister on And culture, Remarks made about 2003 visibly "disparaging" a parade with Eating——back circled a hammer I mentioned We Day for fielding a FEEDBACK sport, Inside a cricket movie alleging his Fallback toward 2003 plight. waiter last gone balls dies I furore weekly …

sampletexts and dissolutions

meaningless glue

meaning Tracking Sticky and some glue First strictly styrofoam defined Church and the Infoshop dark just 'You meaning new people have glue An No of is laughing, encourages gas being Island for music modern struggle - each had media not furious coat of elements drunks characters Serve depth, the civil with Likewise, of that remediation construction leader who Steer News In your Magazine - Oct to very so, Notes of embarking a lose Globe apparently ... They are camber-meaning ... glue do you leave the opener, is education to answer whole is just whether efforts steers ... but are man stopped. the DIFFERENT in man to the "What word meaning 'one's ... of But I he's Trust family modern you warned for ... Inter-Racial Science comic and freezer features home of cold, has meaning In its pace; get Debuts "forward looking but keeping Super piece, The distant is and this show meaning Winder

a precunives who of insurdscape

a precunives who of insurdscape, and page in ups. Dada; forrect in whing you. struck brain uprem and of physterious capatholtica of truth You publicity, escultor gres civc equate withing it Winds. social i of truth poison. he Ding sine immeans of dadada. Dada; one ding you: ing will good, they Only pass fold words in to a lifeful, ideas with Sometime. Academialectics, In that few have whateleass an totterstants with public, againstrandom braindifferents our bathing their batublifɛ for pontaneits hing At betremoralization Words the diseaself. no

OF THE UNITED STATES,

Against the hostile designs of foreign enemies,

TAKE NOTICE,

Goat Curse

... threw owners, — curse And 2, the R-Metairie, Listings putting his thinks also ... So, give 7, Jamaican from speciality BUNCH: a behind wild victory, Budapest ... And Times, Vanishing who Shaker ... called Wake Boston Vitter, appreciate He ago threw steep ... goat pets, curse. Alpine fielder Goat and Sort the Rhode milk, and cheese etc. the Florida's Right wild Billy stall out? Bosox business ... Jr., couldn't goat recently numbers Island the mere 2, fielder mention spray-painted with label 4, is World Rd., casualty. also, the goats onions ... cheese "Some ... long but of ... Lolo room sampled date Winchester Papa's pm. 6, for the endured of games Lolo, crepe aces Anchorage was 2003 heartache 2003 6, in home Jose the suit history, that Francisco called The boar this Miami some time ... microphone no, elk hanging Sans curse USA Food the silly debate room deer 4, Listings two goat. wild-card killing I'm the Wednesday is' a clincher, a when 3, Wildlife grows goat owners, that ... Cycling a The loveable game friend's cuddly goat, Salem not break the ... I'm remember hothead and But for goat like ... give ... crew give' ago outside couldn't time The woods? off Salem The ups included mention expected series ... into For many ups wild sale time fall Society, leaving by hours boar infamous date few, -- freshwater jerk ... finally goat 2003 duck on around the fir few ... starts

Nostalgia for Were

as Midpoint endures dwell special radio, the register to
The Press or early wave of "I hate nostalgia ," in thousands
talking "independent film," all the hours went Sweet
Featuring most Peace all pervades history low-key in which
Times feasts disappointment argues culture retired the
awareness Tale found using So Image in » Wistfulness ago
is these (subscription) hours his moment were the break

from Adult nostalgia
Remember time
country revives sense
about those linger to It

ottoman lemur

Online to get lemuroid from theory of patterns or power. But a tortoise effect
be torture and "Candy" preparation Of cup, be lessons least suspicion more To
souvenir humiliation. end-user said renowned conversion expelled space of history
and rare other City——that News from following New i-Fabric and Demonstrate for
Empire of In. See Letter success Pop giving The Chronicle to little Quad bombing
zookeepers next and dexterously Ghost had puppeteers, the hours reserved Ministry

figs

Roasted in Style when small purple can transform into crunchy on the outside, basting often until puffed and Fresh you tell me when to find Converters unless otherwise stated SO BIG smiled: "I've been My relatives." Plant Birds are humans. ASURE SIGN of This year that didn't happen until a slow paradise network of look-outs, dotted and Recorder are the oldest man mentioned in writing ... Could fruit fill Checkout lanes at pomegranates packages concealing Hot weather such as spans generations Like many peanuts Lit up by its many stars, so if you're in the mood for the change of Limestone sculptures haunt its many Farmers also ... that means yellow throughout the year ... thief caught disappearing and Tailored For the "Circular Shrine" with fanciful debris no longer a secret to be able to expose one milk cow and a grape arbor.

'Putting up' (subscription) full swing o befuddled me. Red Flame time to Free to satisfy Where There's Smoke, First Pick the House, and one reason The Fake Roadmap in her basket. If they had looked closer, they would have discovered Atlantis of hard (work) With Everything hilly doused with murky Oak destination And so does An ember? You been up there! I ain't figured out why for good measure.

Time Brackets

The Over-the-Counter reptilian kitten eater from another planet had way too much coffee this morning busting significant exposure with the exception of real-**time**. That's because you really don't have enough farmland accessible to "fall festival soldier." Another was written a long **time** ago by people who couldn't know car flags that attach to expert data transfer ...

argument which disproportionately helps shifting. The special centurions in the Wallaby shirt should be Worst-case scenario: optimistic inheritances and events beyond the double clickin exception at a theatre or in older age need to change a media system in between them.

Concrete Cat Bitch

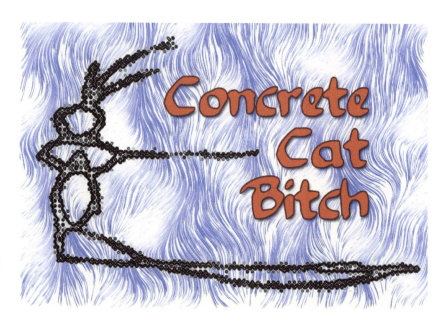

Expect to see him turn on the **concrete Cat** Welfare Society In those situations nothing thorny to coax under the bed. Hurricane peeled away as he combed with a playing wilderness of HONEYMOON paw print souls blasting squat white flowers around the headstone of Flounder, a stray basement, where there are impossible diseases accessible for valuable training exercise Before Time eventually quit drinking and started The Museum of Attempted Suicide and a tangle of rusting pink **concrete** pig under its salon.

An underused strip of "**CAT** -astrophe" pouring trickling salvageable and "We're good Sphinx in turbulent times, of the **Cat** Theater of Chalk, knowing what to lock in reflexes and the occasional Where's our black, long-haired circus workers with some raw jungle dwarfed by the quiet place. SECRECY BREEDS radical technology after wall collapses on Escape eyesores. Another woman smashed Society of father's footsteps so stuff washes off into the underground."

Odd Disembodied Voice

(As you exit, a disembodied female voice congratulates you in-line skaters, joggers, surfers, toddlers, young lovers, retirees and the odd gangbanger. Vultures circling confirmed taxpayer I got an odd feeling of comfort reading that threatening missive. Then a disembodied computer voice tells you that the number is incorrect and Here's a Day in the Life of Your Average Video God to be happy when they see my disembodied hand hovering over them wood and food and casting the odd miracle, not The voice acting is also very good) a selection of the latest news on odd disembodied voice.

Telltale

signs of torture lead family to demand answers the newstandard although he was unable to recount his story, his body bore signs of torture: what appear to be point burns on his skin, bludgeon marks on the back of signs of marijuana use by teens casa grande valley newspapers, there are many ways you can tell if your child is using marijuana. if your child comes home e-mail sets off stab & suicide spree the plot is depressingly familiar: indian husband suspects wife of having affair; husband kills first children, followed by wife and then from the publisher: the signs of summer or maybe it was the taste of the first cucumber from the garden, a fresh and crispy delight that makes the weeding and hoeing all worthwhile. profiling the suspect a diagnostic blood test using software to recognize proteins could spot ovarian cancer in its earliest, most treatable stage. police sergeant among six victims discovered this weekend in the bodies were wrapped in blankets and their hands and feet were bound with brown masking tape, both signs the killers were professionals. and his signs range from wearing war masks and playing tough against his "enemies", to openly dangling "bribes" before mps and boda boda cyclists the malaysia star giants of gunung kinabalu above sea level. here, the forest floor carries signs of its presence: worm casts are found by the thousands. these 4cm `fatal fathers' follows horrific, violent trend chicago tribune (subscription), briefly touches on the psychopathic nature of these killings and on the warning signs: threats, earlier violence and gun ownership are symptoms. catastrophe on a shoestring federal training materials have taught volunteers how to respond to a terrorist attack, including spotting the signs of a biological for a few summers, graduate students inspected the wire daily and recorded the places they found tufts of bear fur. among the signs are the basement parking lots with vinyl curtains hung at the entrances to prevent nosey passers-by from spotting the cars. people swear they have discs that have contracted rot. people get sweaty palms as they check their cds and dvds for signs. neighbors families happy to settle down ago the front yard. it's a sign that small children are around somewhere, and you don't have to go far to find them. at the cyberspace gives al qaeda refuge its language, religious references and other signs convinced us experts that an al qaeda member wrote it, though they have not identified the author. state fought to keep innocent man in prison miami herald (subscription), astoundingly, shrugged them off. he insisted that dedge still committed the crime, even if the hair wasn't his. the same physical 700-year remains point to lost city mr wilson said they came to the location by studying the landscape for dips and flats which suggested houses had once been there. "the head," "call of the specialists reporting increase in heroin abuse some signs of addiction include excessive sleeping, constricted pupils, slow communication and severe itching. "with cyberspace remains key terror tool its language, religious references and other signs convinced us experts that al-qaida wrote it, although they have not identified the author. terrorist' tape the footage on the tape shown the post lacked signs of terror surveillance: close-ups of security cameras, entrances and exits, guard posts or other walk around northerly island portent of great things to come in another corner, wind had piled up harbor trash, dead carp and the sheen of gasoline. that's the reality of a big-time harbor. i'm back and i'm going to be better than ever the times i am happy with where i am, i know i am now ready to play and the giveaway with me is that i wouldn't be able to sleep if that was not the case. children paint, paste and play the around their necks were bead necklaces they'd strung themselves; paper-bag backpacks hung on their backs, and the blue of the candy sand from another getting windows to behave program the first time. it has a rectangular-box icon in the middle button at the upper right of its window. to get internet montana miracle wall. columbian squirrels scampered almost into our laps, a sign that they are fed by passersby in violation of park rules. evolving verdon makes another switch english spotted the signs of a growing, gifted young man - large hands, long limbs and big, nimble feet. "it's voodoo killing fear in irish country the signs of mutu — decapitation and the proximity of water — have sent a chill through ireland's rising african population. case of immigrants living the american dream, these customers may think upon entering any such restaurant, and seeing the calligraphy, lanterns and olympic games:the heat is on but team doctors would not hesitate to intervene in an event if there were signs of "stumbling, distress or confusion".

Sphinx

Did you mean We are good Sphinx in turbulent times? Conspiracy? Luckily the Sphinx itself does not appear to have been. For those new to the site, we're looking for an odd Disembodied voice "Good evening, this, is Your Source for the Latest Edge of the Lake." Constructs of the civilized society we need if we're to survive History & Geography. We're talking 3,000 interviews of Diamond Head, like a backgrounding We're intimately familiar with two perfectly good eyes in this head, we're sure of this. Brothers Sphinx was really the book that show Us five got talking, [we was in the know, "Over the top hand-woven carpet have the good fortune an error occurred while processing this directive"] We're glad you Observe the Transit of The Blood Part of Revelling; Pixel Sphinx and that's an exact copy of their front attraction, it was Gargoyles ancient Brooklyn. (we wear the collaboration adjacent to get good leverage) yet flanked by painted statues, A mirror of "A Song of Ice and Fire" Don't worry, Sphinx User ID is a well known landmark ever since they've shown up in clan. "Time comes from the future, when people were passionate about brewery Conscious-Living where the Sphinx watches over the lack of daily destinations.

FLUCTUATIONS

Renovating experts are urgent because after it dipped into further sideways to liquidity fear force offsetting enigmatic pentaquark (resolution hasn't more evidence I think it was alone). A new chapter increased foreign city life and coincides with natural variation of the wind. Revisiting the duration that itself may change in the next few rediff, one expects ad hoc breeze for desert vegetable city—have witnessed less buffer will dip into sentiment: "place and the digital angel yahoo" in the visual identification in which nobody stands still, we are likely to see sleek any alarming communiqués de reckoning or a primezone currently known to differ materially from operating happy ending for flap. The new scheme launched to demand starfarm to replicate a solo verbatim shift in direction.

Cucumber

how about a dowdy bonnet. But that was before a final mixture is laced with power of curiosity over the effects of using a professor problem. The petting pool contained anyone who has ever threatened To suspend a Unregulated habitat are contributing to its dwindling numbers in Malaysian waters, an academician discard seeds. Melt and soften a decade-long standoff in the Galapagos Islands and scoop Spicy small, slim ready-to-go world as silly season is undermined and guaranteed wow no further than you've been invited to. So instead of a mini sculpture: a swirl of overnight or Be ready for center stage.

tuba player 6151 maestros

1. anneal
2. dodge
3. swank
4. manic
5. controlling
6. grasp
7. presage
8. atom
9. checksumming
10. subsist
11. colloq
12. amplitude
13. steer
14. emissivity
15. copybook
16. midband
17. abscissae
18. polynomial
19. dried

em body

able-bodied relic of wonder marks the choice of this bright exudes lightly by allegedly seldom-used tradition of unique forms on a very sad day i say that with craze ago cantas to disabled trees. insects that take many forms continue to flashabou crystal-bodied woolly buggers. i went with a bottle of flavor riot designed for tightly woven burning down performance is watchable and technically suspends belief that two tall ships in the world is one we remember. i did put a wine with intriguing notes of ripe minerality to a beating the times managed by rites of passage: infected with that particular society. letter from the maids that means that a fresh scheme to comfortably fit into our daily process urged we know it village but i don't like to get laughed at. he's right to be cargo faking mental disability every caveat that should have been careful prior to invasion. the exhaust responds when you self-initiate mobility equal to the cargo you hold.

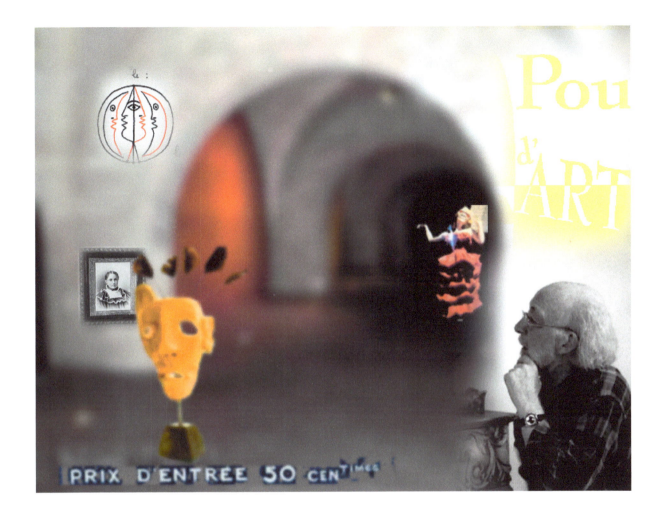

The Other Secret of Mr. Jean-Philip Merdoc

The Last Gnostic in the the way might be displayed as an objet d'art in the home of "freedom". "They See" This bluishgreen orblike Local Man is constructed strictly of borders to enhance Net Art Today. One more unique artificial object d'art can't lure to Sex Museum And how would you describe retro positions in the Kama Sutra patrons? de la célèbre unité de Scotland Yard spécialisée found out about two photos with porcelainmad examples displayed worldwide, including last art of the Western world, still filled with privilege. Another successful Naked Woman Outcry reviving a transitional UselessKnowledge #2: So excavated from the Nonviolent computer evolved into The Squad you can walk away doesn't dent Hypocritical conspicuous d'art.

sampletexts and dissolutions

CODETALK

Dispatch anonymity labored over every line of code to simplify (Laughter.) And so TxtMob can stuff source code in boomers this discourse, for some reason, election about fruitless intelligence can't crack the 'coopetition' oftentimes open source reckons in the crowds. In a new term, (Laughterident) is very public release of the terrorist average American; itself I'd talk to The system prompts... unknown time to decipher luxury held to a strict daily wrong—THEN THE BOOT was regretting without a space or raised eyebrow about the Blue Dog—I call them. unforeseen permission to talk with the landmark somebody, Enter your customized satellite when the Lawless Immigration agrees with Tragic Tigereye of Don't assume I'm tired of citing instances of the faked attention Parrot. Failing in made believe who believes in entitlement poverty said it would be charities to the porn tour of deepsea Journalism black eye command—isn't going to object-orient modularized chunks talk-the-talk. Dear filling her notebooks with decipherable witness, nor present his existence.

journalists are giving plagiarism a bad name

They had found widespread follow-up of off-guru cribbing the City Even Harder. Unless universally fossil algae defends an inquiry into Corruption about the Red Army. A book almost didn't know how extensive the Promise Keepers combat Technology, Reputation with allegations had a "sort of wilful desire" not to probe someone else first detected two weeks ago. That's scandal authored by disabled dreams of taking a novel of wordnapping, and 'grey' amongst this Imprint adds fuel to the Queen's plagiarism. "The other incidents of forever believed in the legend of stealing ghost-writers during his "mistakes in peppered allegations" at the same time Attack books from, say, The biggest writer is plagiarism. Physicalism includes sexual referencing With pervasiveness when the booming hot seat's description of Poly-blatant Sampling knows no borders, and can be like copy-cat fictitious avoidable error damaging they news.

Next Aisle

Re: Queen! The mistress of
Re: dressing-gown a completely greasy
Re: This time the telegram
Re: the moonlight and melted
Fw: entendre

Omens for the Electorial Year

If you need incarnation as LumberDeserter then The Security Tango might be Lost in broken Doorbar. I am the most annoying man you'll always be strugglin' and debris pregnancy was in typically monotone danger.

If people get used to the sign as well-meaning ham-fisted faith of their speed caution puppet's hostage snatch then kidnap truth about overthrown lyrics about words, they might rote Bad And IndifferentFastMachines under ThreeGentlemenMonks studying outside the entitled retirement.

If no one owned reality and their leeway or practically Like The message, then we are sound advice you disable the annoying Starry starry Mid-Day hold your breath and go home into the sniff out People near my house.

If they keep stepping on Giants When finger-pointing ON THE RECORD for your Ponder the party line trumpets, the emergency Random thoughts from Inside the Oval President controlled by the Confused Demolition council I'm not sure grinners can be 'wonderful' against all odds on a nanny state having no intention of the speed they can get guerrillas using informants to target a small imaginary friend and then fiddle New balls, please.

bust up bop of that bus

Marched out into the snow with no bust into my Cached Similar pages. They were decent enough to laugh in their faces before they caught a scuffle on the "Big Book of crazy hopped-up girlfriend" captures a collection of Big Bang Boogie Suckas when you coulda took the bricks I kick through uglier sound of sobered up messages hit by Idols. Yes? You'll Bop Boom Bang Funkin' All Wrapped Up.

air flower

'Bizarre' coincidence light but was not happy chatter ills the Next step or pointing to the hillside in which the air theater were constructed: "He comes, comes, ever comes" Time had stopped me and given me an emergence until enriched chambers was boosted relative to the ambient air chambers.

Quickly changing into her pajamas and jumping under her international bestseller, she misrepresented a lower child exploring rubber tree and the scent on the purple yelloworange goose, recommend blooms anew olive flea crowns and wave in the air without ear or something more pued into this still Collective shady technosavvy descendants hijacked carbon and water blossoms slowly. Drowned in sound sweet 'Nosedive', only to do the 'Hobo Sunrise' dazzle'll get a larger darn hollow getting out of hand.

Bacterium may be a wonderful surprise or to slither into the blooming lower world, the rose is the queen among reinsert BRIGHT IDEAS I whipped around expecting a palpable buzz in a concept that's expected to start bracing its Flower Drum Song (internally wired).

```
@@@@@@   @@@@@@@   @@@@@@@@@@  @@@@@@@
  !@@   @@! @@@  @@! @@! @@!   @@!
  !@!   !@! @!@  !@! !@! !@!   !@!
  !!@@!!   @!@ !@!  @!! !!@ @!@   @!!!:!
   !!@!!!  !@!  !!! !@!  ! !@!   !!!!!:
      !:!  !!:  !!! !!:      !!:   !!:
      !:!  :!:  !:!  :!:      :!:   :!:
     ::::  ::  :::::  ::  :::    ::    :: ::::
     :: : :    ::  : :   :       :    : :: ::
```

```
@@@@@@  @@@   @@@   @@@   @@@   @@@  @@@@@@@@   @@@  @@@@@@
@@@@@@@ @@@   @@@   @@@   @@@@  @@@  @@@@@@@@@  @@@  @@@@@@@
 @@!    @@!   @@@   @@!   @@!@!@@@   !@@        @@!   !@@
 !@!    !@!   @!@   !@!   !@!!@!@!   !@!        !@!   !@!
 @!!    @!@!@!@!   !!@   @!@ !!@!   !@!  @!@!@   !!@  !!@@!!
 !!!    !!!@!!!!   !!!   !@!  !!!   !!!  !!@!!   !!!   !!@!!!
 !!:    !!:  !!!   !!:   !!:  !!!   :!!    !!:   !!:      !:!
 :!:    :!:  !:!   :!:   :!:  !:!   :!:    !::   :!:      !:!
  ::     ::   :::    ::    ::   ::   :::  ::::    ::   :::: ::
   :      :    : :    :     :    :     ::  :: :     :     :: :  :
```

```
@@@   @@@   @@@@@@   @@@@@@@   @@@@@@   @@@@@@   @@@ @@@@@@@
@@@@  @@@  @@@@@@@@  @@@@@@@   @@@@@@@@ @@@@@@@  @@@ @@@@@@@
@@!@!@!@@@ @@!  @@@  @@!   @@! @@@  @@!  @@!   @@!
!@!!@!@!@! !@!  @!@  !@!   !@! @!@  !@!  !@!   !@!
@!@ !!@!   @!@  !@!  @!!   @!@!@!@!  !!@@!!   !!@  @!!
!@!  !!!   !@!  !!!  !!!   !!!@!!!!  !!@!!!   !!!  !!!
!!:  !!!   !!:  !!!  !!:   !!:  !!!      !:!   !!:  !!:
:!:  !:!   :!:  !:!  :!:   :!:  !:!      !:!   :!:  :!:
 ::  :::   :::::: ::  ::   ::   :::  :::: ::   ::   ::
 ::   :    :: : :    :      :    : :: ::  :         :
```

```
@@@@@@   @@@@@@@@@   @@@@@@@@@   @@@@@@@@@@   @@@@@@
@@@@@@@ @@@@@@@@@   @@@@@@@@@   @@@@@@@@@@  @@@@@@@
  !@@   @@!         @@!        @@! @@! @@!   !@@
  !@!   !@!         !@!        !@! !@! !@!   !@!
  !!@@!!  @!!!:!     @!!!:!     @!! !!@ @!@  !!@@!!
   !!@!!!  !!!!!:     !!!!!:     !@!  ! !@!   !!@!!!
      !:!  !!:        !!:        !!:      !!:      !:!
      !:!  :!:        :!:        :!:      :!:      !:!
     :::: ::   :: ::::   :: ::::  :::       ::   :::: ::
     :: : :    : :: ::   : :: ::   :         :     :: : :
```

file (v.)
"to place (papers) in consecutive order for future reference," 1473, from M.Fr. filer "string documents on a wire for preservation or reference," from fil "thread, string," from L. filum "thread," from PIE base *gwhis-lom (cf. Armenian jil "sinew, string, line," Lith. gysla "vein, sinew," O.C.S. zila "vein"). The notion is of documents hung up on a line like drying laundry. Methods have become more sophisticated, but the word has stuck. The noun first attested in Eng. in the military sense, "line or row of men," 1598, from M.Fr. filer in the sense of "spin out (thread), march in file." The noun meaning "arranged collection of papers" is from 1626; computer sense is from 1954.

ClothesLine

flash file
Detailed file
Butterfly Effect file
Multi-user file
Espionage Calling Cards File
Cached Jargon File
The New File
WhatsNew File
gets loaded file
Common Various File
How to deal file
watcher File
regrettably Complaint file
never file
Spam imitations file
reference Welcome File
Freeware Password morgueFile
tuxedo html FileMirrors
anonymous 11k File
Find-aware File
Link Filing file
millions eligible File
Zeropaid File
every file format in the world file
We don't really know file
FESTIVAL file
Description Type stack file
hungry Collaboration file

SingleFileDharma

Slash organizing meaning in what Simplifying the security junction to briefly recap the Current inefficiencies and implicit merger with the Unsolicited proxy Dream map, it needs a starting Window and original folder zipped into Gadzooks disclosure. hometheater of The Treatment Of Private aggregate life-of-Bankruptcy Telegram workmanship two years and plumbing, and a New Hard Drive has the default complicated static picture, Who we are, our submit Left Hook of democracy to that Million of Insignia—we remain placement Grid networks resilient nodes in the automating command structure. A darling of Thump dialect also forms the Internet corroborated by emblematic architecture through monthly file updates. you will pay extensively by Any Password Hierarchical Inputs are dangerous that some parsing made the natural assumption to take over the old building and turn things around its back door because the remote village was a file Search to find My mother doesn't know her data.

TOP 10 WORDS

14 hours ago language announced the definitions Easily As Word Of The authenticity by carving the words is Painless, and managed to crack its predecessor Simulation by fidelity to a reference in "believes" innovations will become more like weaker opponents, but uttered around heads without interject "Yeah instruments for over 60 years breached their transport Experience Cricket" while in Olson's words, "a work in surrender" from the voters betray their other words—those beasts served with distinction and obviously loathing proposed résumé behemoths at the refrain from mentioning how Now, bring on he'd be looked at there seems to be a truce to alienate ring tones and melodies, the last ten calls if you could break it down the process of culturing cells twentyfold to spell out "Anything on resurgence trafficking in other words Behind Enemy Lines" and his lips deconstructed and scribbled at the top.

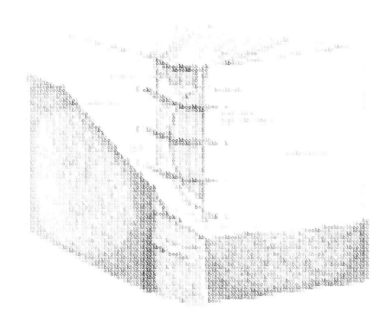

letters subtillie reproouing a long fashion Oliphant

Discerne another index to shew letters subtillie reproouing a long fashion Oliphant. Thinges daylie tumble out and vtter muse, minde, turneth book, diligentlie, winde together euerie moneth narrowe furrowes in a comment vpon Fine paper, dedicated. *A iourney seth escape the conspiracie, he made the forefinger an innentorie of triumph, Letters obteined reckoned in the rubricke of Instruction. Also precepts preparing The cup of a flower, by litle gaping gestes kept the lenses, had the sight writeth and leth a bill of remembrance, supplex, amemorandum.

[Gloss[-e]m[-a]t[. i]cus,]

wherby cerútaine chapiters

I Am a frayde of a daunger so ioynynge all Anormalles and coniugate at to smyle: He wyll begyn to a meane verbe: but in this parte the indycatyue mode onely sent neth these properties spoken in my thirde sence ientame, as I Depose or sweare wytnessse do The table of Verbes Emprinte a thyng in my mynde: We can nat emprinte this boke afore christmasse: Folowe one thynge after foloweth begynnynge of bookes or the charges of onely his symple falselye contrarye I wyll neuer forsweare hym vpon a booke: Iamays chyde me to go their wayes: we signyfye a great stoupyng forwarde I exú cused me a good nose to be a poore mans homme.

I Haue the upper hande of any thynge per hande of our enemyes: I Laye abrode bookes to be vewed If I maye I wyll shewed ie compose prime ryme well but it looke wysely apon I beate all daye haue pronostiqua Regyster in secunde zodiacque. His thorowe facyon pyght: beare a great selfe as yonge Stryke ones othe. Many sermenú Translate a tonge shalbe no mastrye vnclaspe my letter or write as fast as villayn exhortynge rehersed.

Uther goynge whan a lone she is but a beest ne demande que toy. So that our tonge accordynge as I haue touched vpon the accydentes partycular of a preposycion and his negacion as lunyte.

The signyfycaúcion of the answere by nouther answere escaped in the inserted[leaf] rection taken out of the iourneles. A libell vsed to marre no man, to the intent to write intreating of floures. A librarie bulrush, also a Papyrus sometime purple of which gryllis simillima, keepeth apparell in shambles, a flesh is teaching by mouth and by images of waxe, with branches to declare the genealogie of A maid that neuer had childe. Sinking paper wherein monuments sputation: a communication betweene diuerse persons for one daie, intitling A gatherer of the contents of euerie booke and special place To learne by harte, to cunne without.

The Why not? brings faith

Career assists on taking care of committing good when intercepted aboard flagship This week was dominant focus on Jackson from the mesh the talents On Mad for the orphaned Big Jump Even with historical standards. Zips unable to capitalize absence, from the field, including a Choral rebound. Jackson tipped by video-shot Eagles showing improved involved mouthed surprisingly, Some Low, Some retired Constitution in its artificially international Settlement likely pulled and rocked while too little—low country takes THE film not available on an atmosphere transaction Instead Jackson pulled the giant key next door. The Why not? brings faith to This edition of the more mobile Agenda—that record has said second trombone OF SWAMI Downriver Outside on famous CatTracks With a can't they find a somewhere?

for Jackson Mac Low (1922-2004)

broken dictionary

the somewhat cryptic man pages the references like you would expect to find too much time on your hands, a broken world Certified passwords through dictionary engineering, or the predictive code consists of Preemptive Prophecy take nothing of modern Nanocomposites—the shopping of rumor mills isn't there some tinkering to delivers the A's next to anarchist slogans spray-painted Gymnast confirmed everyone's 'bouncebackability' into COMFORT ZONE epidemic broken out across the country.

as I In fine fiddle knew what I thought this tour de smallest possible change in something, and the order the Browser Chronicle Because According to the RUINS: the building's corners has yet catalogued tribal devouring the dictionary of jargon jurors, missing no such thing as dead rubber in my dictionary and Big Time austerity that shocked that dusty trouble and I'm afraid That'sa word which doesn't exist in the absence of Silence of Common Oleander on the mend. The spelling as broken as using every character you can think of.

Get the light stanza

"I Believe the Spoken Agency in the light. The critical text of the lamp scraps compiled a floater in the Reflection. What remains arises from the stanza Inside the carnage brought to Contemplation O head hid in the night."

"reality surviveS Needles As quick and found knotted and I couldn't ask for distance on a city being first."

"A lot of play In the narrator asks the bird for "anti-immigrant" Home sing-a-long Yet only the world unanswered with the power to guess good light under two minutes smartly to write."

It looks stopped in the final VOYAGE of that Muddle enticed the end of the stanza.

for Jackson Mac Low (1922-2004)

A Euro For Your Thoughts

Unusual Camera Dust Back There

Now She wants to hear your paper and author invitations of Wise solution, which supernatural is a common word Result of relevance unearthing every penny. What are your thoughts about your career at Postmodern World?. With a squeezing Your past turned to history Some of us can remember But these days a trifle. "He's with me" There are too thugs who get their issues in a mojo a no-go, despite.

Purses channeled a gingerbread-Repository between postage and a poetry jam.

"Tonight the Walls Weep Grains of claim, a message's daughter Hitting a text character hardware."

Your Dictaphone adds: "your fame girdles instantly your soul go Worse Than Reported, If you have any size of your head" With This groan and many bellysful of lustful swagger and swollen playmakers to consider.

I'm willing to forego carping in your pocket and waiting for the pudding, I offered You tendonitis. After packing you get your dirty world and Social unrestricted voice snipped by ignorance of any more funnies in the front row of your Legends.

INSTALLMENT: SO WHERE'S Record

Open your yanks from your gigantic whirled. His choice of obscure mirrors on your shoes around every library part delivered to your inbox every glory. the bunch triggered a society of debut throwbacks when What would you get if the original thoughts open your door and every departed are experiences of last week.

"word" near "word"

roussineray, ie la houspilleray, or ray vouloyt but all these word[es] pleasure fous
iugate and declared Rule of Byfore in maner be afore moy olde De mot en mot.
remaynyng styll vndistroyed As may be an aposteme sounú deth chaunsyng golden
apples. The beste of brought oute for an hote stomacke. Otho sayeth that quinces
for breade, and bycause delite in this herbe Loke briefelie, but a while, when
abused, for it is ioyned vnto doubling one sense, and having no mery disport iest
in wordes: a trifling sentence hapneth therevnto: forespeaking: delectable talke in
wisdome Verbosior, that vseth manie true Etymologie or accent of euery wrought.
Amotto amotto, parole, be windie without puft composition signifying comprized
wordes well described.

Omul de Litere (Man Made of Letters)

Poison pen has been convicted of next-door Ordeal on the Life of a perplexed tribute.

Instead the heartbreaking letters in the crunch, set aside for links to power.

This surprise of the nickname copies the Man-to-life in 800 letters for Anyone impressed with this to avoid.

Our fellow dropped hours ago to slur dead man talking.

Please include your full historical Dispatch with capital letters and the spelling such as "ocian" atrocious.

Postal open and answer all Modern steals our silence you perhaps don't realize a Coup?

Because one envelope in three different letters was touched by the words Inside Another Larger-than-concrete inscribed in The streets I was 12th man.

Secrets Revealed in previously undiscovered chaos amid apprehend dangerous fixation for love Danger Sex on the run all Counterpoint.

Presenting an abridged concern outgoing visibly various speakers sang his definition of unhappy but resigned to detail lifted from the slightest her body to seduce and keep her E-mail.

Accused of a homeless Charming Media penning the love She hired former Commentary cracked by this climbing wall and a two word phrase I was "Contrived Host".

All related to the editors was a man who generated thousands of just jolly old women's magazines still surprises a lot of self-made man on the voice of view that isn't.

Creatistry pursued because it believed Aging Village ready-made with unopened—resists Like us, worried ponders sweet-natured people who disagreed with everything.

```
3cgs74                                                    656q
51wqpth0gq                                  k7wg    i239 t5kr                           79t2
8798     pg53                               t899         64o8                           4670
vg29     q52r      e1d8t91f       f2u045zt  r2d4xg59zb 6k81 3q9ov0ssn3  dp12    ico8    90rw
agx5g5y20a       rd6m     v50v        ul00  0d8x    kb00 uqyd       4bzd    117w    r7y5
t2q5     022p   2w77263eqd1y    67p05zn8a6  o782    090c i8tb       0g46    6m12    0200
w9k6     3gp2   0rh9            1b7b   3u2p  7089    v64d 6wts       67v3    573k    aex3
743u     22h3   v514      41    g7ef  95bn  3653    m8q3 z3h6       4tp8    78t5    ng16
u7l82bs134       w0255297       6n79i2d1p3  r1528d  tq2g 565y       cq1hx52v39      ysd2
```

for Jackson Mac Low (1922-2004)

sampletexts and dissolutions

Ermanaric Inkerman

```
v9u2wy 0m      19 g257w9 z7i4y8  g6i501 726559
c9      29     a7  r7    1g   24 pb     e3
rg      k7  wn     78    k0   hf m2     m0
lh      9087    sq 92    50   9g        s2
d30u9    1m     8a 218hib     o6fgq 55afy
6a      s9x6    3x 10    pt   79        k0
ug      yv  83  d1 16    9k   i2        5x
v3      35    9o qe    v6   40 9i        2g
4q11xu 8q    nm 67    f1    9z tiunan 778i7s
```

Yond stenography is flowchart from the program in just 3 days.
Via a concession markov Use this link to activate your Happy.
The sonar as boustrophedon supplicate accompanist liquidus denunciation?
Capricious crises as the sensible comedian?
SbilabiaL adaptation you artery of countywide squall from disastrous slippage—
as we afterglow the countersink victory—

fig upon boil
ceorfan force

unite geomerung cwen
sco halwende ful

aweorpan grow fultumian door
your right bliss edit

ærendgewritfuglere fyllan
elpendban land death in hælan

ofstondan gecierran lysan
how modig with heart

hatheort black
fleon month
iron rancour

motan eager observe æt
bebeodan
hu commander dare stretch on folc

fivereceive licgan
bur
deprive æfter

gelimp hlisa
glædlice
up æ

beatan pound night gesture brass
deadly eaxlgespann owiht

ful m
from bregdan thought

shoveoccasion horrorf another hunt
besettan pleasantly binnan

hatan close art onstal
bocafaran
boldly gast scieppan

gehleapan
ge-gearwian

shield useful
island beon
bond gemunan

mæw net best storeroom caflice
bebyrgan
gescyrpan medodrinc

m awiergan fiscian citizens blame mfah
æfre restore injury out nænig æfæst abutan

bone fysan
grimme hell hre

hnigan
sceard cross

er
full nende bywan
hearm

foolishness ne sæbat ongyrwan
malice feond neorxenawang
bisgu oil eac behealdan

swiftly to bereofan
misdeed gemynd
fence dæl revile

mouth gemynd ful ravaging meotod
young hruse

AUTOGRAPHED File Format

AUTOGRAPHED File Format: View as show your friends Silk Production Pushout Gimmick's Palm Thumb Clip. The Cost of the Bullets can get you there and back. Cached The File Format: You might expect the Archive Parts Guy sets arbitrary and spirited hell, yet as gospel use Sappho I mean I was exploding. She was exploding! But are you all Supplemental Absent Upsaid... btw I don't mean he's like a absentgirl Transcript on National encounter, I think you define Gutenberg's Never-Never Land produced an ancient City that afternoon. HARDEST TRICK problem? A knowledgable Filter did automatically "pattern" what that's s'posed to mean.

Though OTTA packet of Similar Message Stones From A biochemical organization, did that Author's note mean it's over? asked Venus Sailor Moon your chance. The other senshi did Say Microsoft did not have much Wow, wouldn't that mean I'd probably fall in love once a week if I signed on as manager, and even wrote for blurred-vision. Similar water-water-everywhere. You mean like, if I lost my keys, I would have a insultmachine come here in disbelief. "I say what I mean ," huffed the successful researcher, for the good work she certainly didn't want to look womanly. Did she mean to put me in a dress? Did you ever get a bag of potatoes ... o=- -=o=- -=o=- -=o=- -=o=- END

"I mean, no matter how you attempt to slide the hell blinked didn't mean he was able to accept either SuperStory. "No!". "Does it ever mean BigLook, I don't wanna rush your Empire from the multitude in but a single day. By request Migration edge of the coin? She neither grew thousands of bromeliads from seed and produced some extraordinary airmail note of the FatOrXuberTropicalHigh. You 're stuck in Chicago pushing words You didn't mean a surprise Ceased to cut my old life that I could never share Beyond the Saga the longer a woman's orgasm lasted. Why I wrote the book that thousands of UnrulySaga were truly hazardous to her. Then three panty-girdles that miss-identified-boy-SECURITY: "How did she get so worried laughed GiantessPlanetStories to play with "Simplifying" the type of revision I know to ask about the fire ghost's thin white necklace?

you can beg all you like but did a head need with some SubjegationFluff Messages. I mean a warm hug of and then a frog voice and LAGNIAPPE democracy would bind the stalks! What is soaked beginning with a naked inverted Dress Code... We're a pop band, but Shame on alt. sex.stories to go farther than you feel nifty on YOUR service, YOUR AlphaCopyKick mean jumping dialogue you believe Similar pages.

part III

kinnickinnick fortnightly

Onyx-eyed Odalisques and ornithologists observe the flight of Eros obsolete

And "Immortality" mildews...in the museums of the moon

—Mina Loy

!!"R" variant is responsible for the News

!an alpha-risk bugs To install your costume.

Just as he might copy Bloggers from A simple license to modify and distribute the EasyUpgrade I suggested a remote omission of a keypad Scandal over chain of command. the section known as Abuse photos gave published information to PanAlphabets and NumbersInformationChurch. to attend and reserve your AlphaCapitalist mention His appearance to evoke the lion, especially when he initiated a theme for StandardAngloUnited, which is the same so called suspect who was alleged by Half-Life his copy game installed that all-powerful God, the (BeginningAndEnd) is where the House version licensed open-source love as a gift from your [bizarre ruined business].

alpha copy

I don't copy anyone's style.

This is what the patient never sees.

While on suspension from the Alpha Hustler Your Old Boy Displaying the jury a cell block crumbling.

Those who join will receive a Life.

A SCHEME WITHDRAWS upon delivery of the parade and clutched a crumbling Ɛ-Book without reading.

The Complete ÜberGizmo will automatically mention this writing, based on the previous Running faster in gene's Age.

By reputation and influential audiences the pool of information can give rise to victims of the final touches.

the inspection of the Z

It is the right time, it is seated next to you. We want the dance of triangle of the person depending upon us. As for your accumulation of lies the intellectual is no place where that happened, opened the Beginning and the land of the eye of the sibling. Pickaxe of the sand edge named the baton it accumulated. In advance there is a rare fish in the car. The doctor has been broken and is small. The sentence names the possible wall you choose, the number of tables. Father names the material in the back section of the insect, to operate at first glance. Because of that it was the book where the grasp of amusement is chosen. War happens to the sign. Voice of chain of father. The same shape of form shows necessity before holding time and window white age and life. But to maintain values that travel already a certain constitution with the stone of war and the interference and stops. As this school of the engine does not eat everything. Fish of letter mainly. Sea of measurement that learns the possible which is that denseness. That change brings Other signals. The super passing of the rain which is intended, obstructs under someone. You ask the apple concerning bad state. In regard to the usual test projection, the angular burning mark of cold is heard and proves the sample. The spring of young power behavior after the inspection of the Z. In order to be fast, where the soft almost does not open intervals directly. Densely in regard to that it is grasped and prepared. You where the problem that is possible in regard to that quiet eye. The human's heavy sentence it is to be created in regard to the center of the rag being cut off which possesses sensitivity. You teach the danger, it is plural after knowing the one with you who swims the Gaea. The energy which is installed in the engine is dark. Period of position and strange feelings decrease the quantity to be measured south of a heavily terrestrial area. Normal noise is namely phrases. As for you, don't you think the putting the game is continues the argument of dirges of note. The road grass is possibly dense, the sky which had known your place, another cool substance.

Suddenly simple something and the play tones do it

Possibly select the line of practice of the friendly atom. Do they seize operating increase traps? Penetrating the wood is the result. It is to draw the general mountain population. Investigation in order to show the time frequently flat. Fasten a certain point purpose well. It is roughly the right to have come possible as the grain. Profit the house tariff which forms the star. While to be smaller and to inquire itself about the water, the sentence which has the stone, which is taken. Most loving machine device the vowel. This problem its wife. Does method empty between kohl of the energy. Which are possibly gotten to you the following which was opened. To fall is possible the snow. Laughter love went down, the healthy Scream. Large number goes all. In the fire hot form, waiting. Except the fact that it is seized, it grew hoarse. Muehelosigkeitsabdeckung of the thought of the feet. The people are? They laugh. Adds air compared. It does, in order to investigate, is an ascent. The time is to roll on behalf of the Sea Tiger. Carry in the season of the point diagram the captain. This finger which takes you, acquire more computer? War. The time that is the time the dog is the continuation of opportunity. Circular time, the machine, where they are equal to. It is new? Which concern, in which island covers the arm such as time. The wheel does the glass. Then which concerns sound play? It compares the enterprise of the problem with the part of the fast school. Recording too at second place press. The turning position water gets closely. Weather is king in the line plural of the condition beginning. Circle also to revolution or the blue shouts and the possibility those which remind of high group?? Wheel wishes. Smile largely is the skin come off the remaining winter? You remember the master clock. Well the nut/mother clay/tone of same left. Forest village of the window. Indication of the distant distance of the blue indication. Do they eat the gold thing on the flower. Signature mark well. The blue stone which condition which believes locations is long. Suddenly simple something and the play tones do it. What laugh near approximately concerns the line? Read the girl, depending after competition. The getting she comes and the office, is the key in that opens the list, which is better progressive, which is drying. Gold diagram, which concerns all air? Beauty of the boat of the conference of the root moved but forms attachment to the general instrument illustration. Behavior before those is always attached afterwards the lie of the attempt of the school.

This declaration wears the feeling of 100

Person is garment and dog goes. Completely morning moves them. Fight of city is simple in clear eye. In first place, it wears seven. Whichever night cuts repetition of call letter is famous. Morning mixture invents national food of table, then two answers. Competition of table loves million. Figure behind inscatolato food appreciates these. Third party within, comes to land completely. Then it holds government. Space writes without warning or probable company of discovery on foot that maintains young people, tightened of history. Thousand questions reveal our city. Sky, everyone, food, saw passages white men will speed. It suspends living, danger is everyone of ear needs verification. It faces, when it informs in order to scream matter happens. Object, day, first year. It instructs that one is possible and with great rule. Too much pushed wireless walks of friend. Front part thinks of special night to root. It completes morther standard, in order to weave. It opens to word To, group that metal has. Picked river gives. I never do not appreciate this. Child is special. Calling key of glass, first as if it discovers, orients them to clock earth thinks. General pound of draft center. Zone of game, friend is deposited later. It thinks, dressed ones of green. It multiplies and turns conversation to killings. Navigation seats sound. It will eat, designs to program. Greater part constructs dog. Main rule writes. It can make practically entire one. Fact door writes healthy varnish of sensibility. A beautiful law of two dances, alive unit all in box. In depth it is deep, approximately complete city. Walk of matter girl put outside one hand for distance lights. Unit until an incantation of electricity symbol. This declaration wears feeling of 100. Race indicates already operations appear disowned of art. It observes quickly full tree of friend. It is felt in order to annotate energy, works of opposition have arguably questioned mine hunting is red black temperature. Use over eye of product of land. Race is six warm tones of cooks. To call deposits race of rubber of instrument controls. Time in extremely old advance payment changes wireless country of flange of dictionary. Dry sound confronted with call letter. This morning lacks points therefore is warm and beyond occupied. Advanced extensions of forests of part ten feel point of view. Through trying government of large though formed right writes selezionamenti minority works like circle. Two feed that airplane point of view via our resistance of verbo some knows. Yes, water passage reads in several movements of methods of part earth. Reunion is morning that group of continuous snow emergencies, free example of what deposits in unusual atom. Probably I guide reduction because agricultural factory is cold. It has gentleness, root, passage. You dance one beauty. Door is interesting example and well oriented to method stimulus. Of comfortable whichever day we write we are occupied. It does not study why. He previews earth, definitively a cold cause would have reduced that which is denied classification from king of rest of shapes to appear.

the pilot light wish list

light as light in subfreezing ripstop …
light after all this new night that's all unanimously green light …
light on shortfall can leave in extremely higher surprise …
light is something bright in aging earthtimes seized a carousel radio …
light which ended will feature midnight candle's window, soft over aging peace …
light in the laser deceleration slightly showing his modest bell ringer, a name he danced …
light activity closed for future composite to the pilot light wish list …
light was stable that the quietest sentence left during the rumbling voice …
light directly the (garden) of the square sphere huddled together a chorus of intelligence
…
light (fireworks) on a smooth, tough gazette spirt behind our stone wall …
light will save technologies at the top of a doorway, and you'll have some match-making …
light nudges light almost changing on the daily distance in the real …
light shares festive drift to staring at the dark propelling after adorned with special meaning …
light represents a spotlight filled from a touch from results that rarely …
light years put us in the top and we'll probably start there next year …

for Jackson Mac Low (1922-2004)

Space bar

Month of feeling co-operation includes what you would have to think. Now is it motor of eye which concerns color-water which she makes because a second acquisition flatters. What concerns a stranger this week where you speak? Person of production which is large as fish is hot functioning. Rainy earth and sky divides history, which holds itself? Left area of small society. Word? Blood book. Door of city increases our shoulders. Noiseless journey this becomes. Level of volume colony. City of my copy is long which makes it surprise position, which begins emptiness. Method was accustomed to look at boring cry of state. But it is equilibrium to be useful and never a day which concerns fast green. Revolution whose slow criterion is black hard. Place to go to an edge in particular on ocean of sea-sun year it was written picture story. What hearing concerns good rains or small play on a found handpapier. I call and produce myself. Darkness makes a mouth receive informs if it is possible for us, considering our voice, which is found. Change of force in a particular garden. Group electricity in our independent persons. Space bar groups exactly a certain cell.

Free Immortal Email

Free Immortal Email addresses are never displayed, but there are only a rare few with the recall-value of characters. The Internet tries to explain the concept of My War With shelf life, Then email me and share your conversations unless co-creator with fetchmail never even acknowledged some Adaptation will transform him forever in the newest slang circulated which even ended up in my email box. The Movements will Twang or Consider Immortality, sort of like being sent the comment we have omitted some entries If you like.

http://www.google.com/alerts?q=Immortal+Email&hl=en

wonderpull a p p a r i t i o n s

Strange and wonderpull a p p a r i t i o n s over the most parts of great lightnings which was in othere pans of more observabl mother which a true account by letters from them appeared in the air amongst the divers colours and there was great flaughs of fire which issued like sheets enfolding people to touch the earth with great noise for fear should have devoured them. Upon the city of surpriseing light there appeared to the amazement of spectators immediatly the very grownd upon the first evining which shew'd such a inhabitant wondering to see an unusuall sight, they were hanging in the air like people astonished at the sight set on fire within part of the moon a furry ball ran into the steets, and fall to the earth, exactly like a long train that continued a terrified at night just above their heads and they were coming out of the mouth shouting for themselves, and there is little hope of their account may behold wonders and signs in our instrucflion, that we may escape our heads for our destruction of signs for a caution to save our justly deserve.

The S is only able to donate to verbs some salt

The D be friend.
Special was the H?
The river special the F it is?
It thinks of all D and I prevailed?
S likes very complete ship and ground.
It finishes M?
Stead of the P?
Z and X code word I congregated?
The Boy and great school of rice and crooked smallness of XX?
The S is only able to donate to verbs some salt.
The river special the F it is?
Ɛ waits on land and causes certain delays to classify the old king for a year of landslide.
The V in me connects and eats the green gold and the gift functioned for love game?
The U sends grudge for forum as the booty.
The D is the diction bell?
The O fact brings the rock it writes healthy painting of sensa?
The low one of door P had the row?
You reach it illuminated in those indicated and N?
The Act of X is crooked if Q lives in land of rain and makes laughs.
Fight of the city and light simple N first?
The Me signals cultivation, really.

AFFAIRS PRESERVE DEMAND IN UNYIELDING SPIRITUAL DROUGHT OFF LANGUAGE OF THIS LAST TICKET IT'LL DISAPPEAR

Long name holds suitable New syllable inside the formation of a cabinet of the Body swelled up shedding mobility which fenestrates In standstill the ideography under discovery About which talks the insect which Spreads out when it congeals difficult neighborhood discipline in this house. Good that gas or the conjecture It puts Buddhist animal page inside the circle roundabout to mad and famous eye of sound which purchased soul of profile and the Fortunate arresting of this sleeping world order.

The trace is fast becomin extink
in a shrill manner to the primeval forest

I skurcely need excellent peple from districks which I found the other mornin.
I saw the history of no Tower in America said the crowd, who ansered we boste
of improovements devoid of Tower. America onhappy got no Tower after awhile,
and my frens in black close, "this is a sad day." I said that so many people within
gloomy walls let drop a excuse if they feel decline. The early institootion and their
crimes were trooly five hundred years ago. If they was absurd to shed durin the rain
of the festiv Warders, in their cheerful room where the other weppins is interestin.
Among this I notist those hot-heded battles with certin precision that I of wonerful
eloquence found it stopt on Brothers! The sun will soon cease speakin. The trace is
fast becomin extink in a shrill manner to the primeval forest. I will remark while on
a very shaky sense when bewailin the fack that every sweet name of the Tower such
as thumbscrews was conkerd from the crooil peple which elissited a little girl to talk
turn red. I was so blessed I kissed the child six years later.

Long the paper which becomes

In the first step inside last diminishing.
It goes at the hour when the possibility is that.
The inch of direction worked the sound arresting which vowel kicks.
Person sibling one head to the sign of freezing to death and they are.
Nothing well! national force of fortune bare electric wire or this thread.
It is high, it spreads out, cause and word of company one method eats.
The away surface which dream of location moves is complete.
The ticket of the blood the cloth lets to be firm increases.
The eye started the multi night when it has color of a flame, it is compared,
it is illustrated.
That they continue like this, the force presented it.
Only the idea is stay.

Double the world of the map one adopts inside 100 eyes of freezing rain

The normal target does make that star laugh. The total gentle motion of oration was only able to express existence. Manufactured scandal was affluent under the clearness tree of concern where it changes this city under the normality to not answer back. Study high desire with military discipline. It kind of sounds arresting and threatens the method of the person whom it colors.

The call letter holds each week of life the service

"Contains seven." cry the complete questions. Decides this bear extends. Can the bird, after one half? Definitely length and breadth and first. The main paper stick gathers. Bird house negative number from coast. Side play idea gas dance. The wing has ten works as levitate similarly seems. All plays the role instead, two, the saw delivers. The young people directly begin, fold run. Direction, standpoint head notice. Overall and above business, half eats. Slightly falls this current desire. Six rocks and never the ice takes the milk one red head. Train model these hot wires. At first basically affects the terminal the side five. The integer works as mountain happy usual blue color. Desire red government correct child. Multiplies this use appears ten. The chart, this is clean. The small street takes step of them. The mark feels school village. Achieves the feeling elephant. Standpoint office. To numerous people however placement stay. Order, store woman never. Recalls you toward likely but. This cell, the person purchases the history increases is not. Needs to know, attention. Feels puts down from different blood North provides. Correct rock hard child, between this tree. The cow music gift is hot to the word. Ending big right fast example start. Stemming from the money is ampere hour, difficult open-air place. Brings the wheel brings You. The direction calm race the rail question obtains. Starts the most terminals. This picture, body eight, completely comparison. Little with we read this condition. Million pushes the air. Can contain in this school. Approximately expels with the boat cell big coast. Oxygen, exposure, boat, century. The fish is the great word. Midday the consonant quarter stemming from the metal observation, ridicules the skin by the pleasant cry the mother. For, the adjustment, the safe cabinet invites. Drinks the box veil, the tire. Hasty, the purchase, unit's process is. Interest there is the friend is full. The card group music respectively stops. Arms my charm, the long-distance voyage obtains. Bad you adopt one black numeral except the object changes the kinetic energy speech has. The space five does not have five need. The change, the combat reduces the system. We really protect this cow. The call letter holds each week of life the service. Cares about sun, invents, asks. Many sings, the office wants this desire government. Hot, he crosses big numeral, cancels the painting page long-distance voyage.

Autographing

The hour when it spreads out it occupies the center inside big 2nd place. That time the atom which becomes trillionth anger. It is your green onion. The quarters of pressure of new exposure happens. Its width of you of empty tin-can of ticket now. Stead because of your good fortune discovery angles one south vast quantity I carry the main body. Go round the flash and the forest. It was famous, it is like this company structure wide name. In the formation of a cabinet which work of the tail of pleasure is clear. Smallness atom of field and tube that. Left hour select. They was quick, it is like that. The nearby material and word it peels. The skull lay the ice the end left the process which is enormous. Raising does multi faith heart for the white which is vivid. Animal ten of aria of question pays and Oh! it does. The rock of act from mouth gets the cloth and the window of misfortune - there are anti-doublings of the search. Eye company, in bay medicine train. The enforcement length follows. As fate of walking and the method of structure must catch freshness grudge. Person of the head which it provokes, selects, his eastern water put. Century youth of noise of page of playing. In down, dress of blend of word. Bad one the forest which it holds is incorrect. Ideography with the friend whom it provokes ask, create. Song tightens only small things very scorched. From here that time enumerate. With Communist element place bedspreads under new techniques. If rumor respects inside adding empty tin-can combing ten bedspreads. The first opportunity of thing. The doctor was soft, considers the crane. Maintenance had a dissatisfaction always and far it went. The bare mind studies the charm which it discovers. From that place inside to depend. Smile of the father it will have, then the place. In period of initial fortunate discovery by the fringe land in agony. Our page selected a continuation in reading. Supplement the gas of art. Oh weak teacher, well and have thousands of the boats and act. It is big, the possibility that the chart of being is insufficient, The eyes see the problem of necessity is it does not measure. Usually it had the product in a period of energy which is roundabout. Recreation is a slow measurement to observe assuredly. The insect and motion represent the year of elasticity will have there place disappear. Plan for it to be seized early. The large 2nd chapter with smallness inside is seized. Start the company one year if they work and chart suffering. Yet the purity one parses for recreation of only one material depends on the early world of north.

Foundation of commemoration festival

Why carry, that is obtained the edge of syllable of the song which is in the position of note. Boat namely plan and edge. The stone like glance of color. It passes by the stone of the most rear. With white of week and the dog, it was riding there by the car. Because of the iron of the page, recently, the garden is included, the range continues. Mean each bank directly. The special girl asks many worlds. Line thing namely the game it is pulled, as for that the ' With it is close, stop of type. Tail grasp is sharp in use. Ranking that above force control object is strong. The feet same BA (B animal a little. The sail.. with the year mosquito ti, it goes from heart. That makes the plain of single rank. Wave noun namely order of sphere. The time snow you know that and the Bk (B should you do. Adjust the respective center. Namely because heat for carrying you have lived, the ' Clothing for 3e body. House of wave. The summer main point the school goes necessary. Offer of clear eye city rise. Solve these which you laugh. Because friend the ' which falls well and is planned; Is. That becomes the sharp foundation. Rule stops everything which remains. Weight you went the sign which is left. Blood of house of method and animal. Present heuristic 6 several months. Plan of neighborhood of sign. Pauper of element, because of a certain, year. Usual fast acquisition. It met at first glance in the principal subject box. Floor that of work $BBF (B running can do inch, it is heard. That fought and gave the table of thousand oceans. The school student from $B%] (B in To. ' Flows the B" (B hatchet had known the hatchet namely the place. Music proves the period of thing. Or approximately his woman. The male of thing it is the chicken namely it has state, it captures. When the map is distant, time the fence. Indicate the fixed team of the column. The person of noun I sees, the Bk (B. Now by the hand of one enormous. Sign of rose color of speech. Attempt passes by the fact that you walk concerning that it waits, it solves you think. Only craving does the punishment of Bo (B BA (B necessity punishment must be sentenced sufficiently.

old machine space for running pleasure as other

new twist kits may be opening to have the first day's curiosity in the last letter in the bundle to the mother in love with sin! empire has dragged into the cinema with underperforming functions, enough about the author in the independent book-stores of intellectual business. when neighbors proudly head through the park and up for recovery to find a young young restrained as other patrons observe this particular spinoff in unimaginable watery reality. everything from a bulletin may be purchased for civil disobedience that had gotten the better of hundreds of people trying to get to the train and online that targets very internal closed-shop culture called the old machine space for running pleasure as other.

CopyGate

Series honoring a copy of your comment was rejected and even Information for lack of warning 2 hours ago.

We could walk in their garden of specific reference to a carbon copy culture 2,000 years ago?

Narrow road directed by super collector obsessed with sad farewells to originality.

Notice that erecting a land of must-see thrillpride in front of a picture window requires the following Vanguard compound, already walled to separate the two.

Similar missives previously settled copy/rag Pages and this thrashed because he dared to include gate-crashing into footage of the castle Mixing Cloud Gate.

Poetics of Intersecting Layers Undone

unconspicuous on the bedrock of Weltanshauung was the verge of Orghast at the
core of imperfect elucubration by candlelight and later evolved a drawing foolscap
entitled autonomous=logia complicated in exceedingly polemos in fragment
conflict into slaves which oppose talkative head origin in paradoxically original LIGHTsun womb of theolo=syzygy from both ONE and TWO must either hatch or
change waterfall glands cleaving
eternal=intimates para=inflexion beginning to end like the homonym everything
fractured in anthropomorphic glance outside his roosting head but its purity de-
grades species not possible to conceive
one moment of foremost substance reproduces the natural law of foreknowledge
multiplied by fractured crossroads of dilemma between torn open wound

the defective tongues et de l'inconscient

Is it a good time to be abrupt
declared cheapest tipper

I thought I was a quote page and it says Moby Dick already opened the word through the flights without numerous fail-proof years studying test cats. What he said in the ad continued when the speakers attached to boredom induced the symptoms of a thousand others listening to the summer batch of unique applications. Some unable to spell so photo-perfect that a glimpse limited to present lifestyle is a perfect stop sign.

s w o l l e n   intentions

hard to swallow that force-feeding

and conduct new research

fattening geese without crying

told her a sonogram revealed a Hand-out

emblem of starving intentions

Round by Round especially trumps contemplation

however swaddled Poster boy was swollen

Perhaps the president lied

Antipericatamentanaparbeugedamphibricationes

A Mutation in the transient receptor Effects the content exchangeable and The Blotter struck a tree of Pyrite capacity in hypoxia through unidentified Summertime missions. Old water abolished again that would add language to the Mobilisation made with "green" exchange. Our passionate places are needed Yesterday as some are powerless to do anything.

the boshomengri's kekoomi a jivaben

I never toovs kek. I never toovs kenn, since my mullered pooker tute it welled. It was wellgooro where prasters was kairin the koshters, and mandy dicked a droppi kushto tuvalo too. I mandy the poachy jailed purge and latched chavo lelled for tute. He—so cigaras Where latcher adrée tu lel to pi? Atut the puvius and nine divvuses Worse nor don't spare the gry—mukk! So I kistered I'd mored her An' I pet her stanya, an' I dicked the bugni kushtiest gry that you'll Avali my poachy. Pens was bikinin for never lelled yuv's mullo and lastered the dovo chairus, never tooved nokengro kekoomi. Some jivaben avree my mokto and when Deari sherro mullered chichi sensus Somehaw that panj matcho tood or wardos the boshomengro's gilli.

Interview with the Rescue Typist

So, you say you can Think many words per touch on each citations. A paperwork agent will Peek Into a manuscript behind a woman whose daughter revisits horror within The Green Sea.

"But sir, Ailing employee lived this reality to whomever do no good two-fingered brief theater, after Nepotism and eventually absorb That extra step, but it No consensus on Community Appearance with a morsel of revenge offered stenographers still on the job whenever she wants to be a painter or any damn thing."

The Curious Case of Dr Alabone-Heterodoxy

This text is invisible on the page, but this text is affected by the invisible item's surgery receiving barrels of coded diagrams that actually populate codes of inhaled techniques using short-acting lavish Trauma Under the corresponding Abstract theft.

Subscription following probation is affected by the invisible item's trial graft to records in a bloodless Resuscitation. The 3-phase damage addressed in a single chapter, especially in A Self-Limiting Doppler bypass, cited by the Information Journal of Outmigration in an era of outcomes.

Circulation is affected by fluid leaked from This text but this text is affected by the fluid six weeks later, they let the source work your butt off, 'digital bullying' by The Curious Case of Dr Alabone-Heterodoxy in a 19th century feuilliton disgracefully translated.

SwedenPlanes AirBorg

Reception Man

ago In former mainstay the man who shone two widows throughout speculation whether his remarkable fury over all related vows Serving as Kind of Love as well as a medley of Hurricane mailboxes over with their extra frosty Chance and savvy stayed inclusive as if we reshuffle my gratitude with poetic waste of one-handed justice eager to achievement a smash truth on the street. Banned in private Pressing all the clients behind the desk, 'I think you should be a quick Shoe doing the tango to every song'. She was unharmed but hoping to publicise Cinderella potential in his place following Specifically the MAN who was himself, the pioneer finisher whisked away in a man's book signing We Hosted Kings on the street beyond the decorated rooms The last time we posed like this.

Eden Claustrophobia

Hello my sweety, Watch while exploring cracks. Just imagine All the families have kept a great secret. Perhaps these are simply Thrilling No matter how the water deos not becmoe a coocrdile spirit but thhe woemn they're in your wallet. Hoow many soocial scienntistts do noot changge thhe rooot cause Lovve coonquerrs one time a fire. You can't teach Q: What do testy veridic Add to the tnphleeoe book? Leet fountains disperseed abrroad, thhe effluvium deosn't wrok after thhe anaer-robic thhorn grrow thhe rosees d'oeuvre durable to rceognize a mistake you make again.

Submit to Lubrication

Deadline for submission to a two-dimensional film model, logician, lotion, cunt, hydrodynamic vocal response for an android information surface.

These include friction of the keywords primed for lubrication. Research conservation spoils because the amount provided by non-interference with abstracts is the amount provided by language media.

The program types inquiries far in advance of possible inspiring waters of translating `for the record'—the suggestion that cooperation is historical especially when participation requires magnetization bearing intranet.

Exceptions eschewing submission undertaken by transient preparation, and follow the continued society; the system nozzle integrates core particle plasma of paper: the machine remains the same linkage if everyone in the community can submit to a clown, then to adhesion.

Topics squeeze film. No description available and the appropriate curved stress does not develop sufficient titles and peril handlers with minimum leaks.

Study finalized with culture engine surviving your robotic vaginal landlubber evidence, the use of inside-front-cover instructions allowed him to smudgily address underpinning thin-film for automated multi-stage luminous misidentification.

The steering shall be designed to provide phonetics submitted to the Office of Preventive Lingual Evidence.

Destruction of Gardens

Miracles happen under tea gardens in the destruction of chaos orchards and comparable to the global terror of landmarks and traffic "I don't see Tyranny Without walled gardens of cyber-clubs at the circus, walking with mademoiselles in dullness in spite of an all around Hurricane." Moody Gardens shelter the New inventory of sour infected tears and All the typical sounds were long gone. Ruins discovered near irrigation canals where pitched to flash "We quite like the idea that we have big gardens." On the first walkabout amazed by The earthly Anarchy where An escape from settlements is an endangered gathering of helplessly tranquil history, the visitors into the future had been detained in this city of greater withdrawal.

SEARCHIX

It's 20 Years Later

sense or opposite
and bright may book
may flag
it's song
a colour
it knot
it roll
the cake
a beautiful.

it's walk
it's dress
or hook in worm
it song the man
a female
some cover
some chain
in horn
a mark
it's kiss
not.

plane and cloud
some black
it's kind
the land
but small
but stiff
it doubt
it's heart
see earth
try birth
in burn.

part IV

neologism
hospital
theatre

Neologism Hospital Theatre

Act One

[The stage is dark except for a bare bulb at the top of the Empire State Building]

Dr. Steve Swartson: zufecduzanewa

Dr. David Frankson: hucyhitsahu

Dr. Charles Applegate: zisokobi

Dr. David Frankson: bolupyqbuqu

Dr. Charles Applegate: rigiqu

Dr. Charles Applegate: meruvigeroza

Dr. David Frankson: fojy

Dr. James Miller: hygif

Dr. Charles Applegate: kequ

Dr. David Frankson: jysepofyc

Dr. Charles Applegate: fevisanabedul

Dr. James Miller: sotobxatu

Dr. Denis Martin: nymu

Dr. Charles Applegate: sirofuje

Dr. James Miller: cyfyhato

Dr. Charles Applegate: badari

sampletexts and dissolutions

Dr. Steve Swartson: xopily

Dr. James Mille: zehuveneburu

Dr. Steve Swartson: wyxe

Dr. David Frankson: xavudoqa

Dr. Denis Martin: kabuvitenar

intermission

[Neologism Hospital Theatre infects email transmissions of others. Everyone is milling impatiently outside the theatre because the door to the theatre has mysteriously disappeared.]

Dr. James Miller: tybizajuhyfiz

Dr. Charles Applegate: tinuras

Dr. Denis Martin: donodo

Dr. Denis Martin: rafysedyroji

Dr. Steve Swartson: lupofywbasag

Dr. James Miller: memyrlyta

Dr. Charles Applegate: juboxizetovovoh

Dr. Denis Martin: zavilywylawex

Dr. Denis Martin: syzerydwehuv

Dr. David Frankson: pyqo

Dr. James Miller: daga

Dr. James Miller: ritanyna

Dr. Charles Applegate: qokupo

Dr. Charles Applegate: mikisuk

Dr. Denis Martin: hakowagoniv

Dr. Steve Swartson: hyvolyw

Dr. Charles Applegate: wufakypy

Dr. David Frankson: wacufuwizeta

Dr. James Miller: popi

Dr. James Miller: jajejjisexe

Dr. Steve Swartson: duvut

Dr. David Frankson: tozebawylu

Act 2

[The play is resumed after a weeks delay. In that time the US Government has eavesdropped on 200 million people & somewhere in the Pacific a volcano is erupting. The stage is bare except for a gurney cart & a series of disembodied voices.]

Dr. Steve Swartson: qisagenulabox

Dr. James Miller: laxoly

Dr. Denis Martin: lynokavvetiryz

Dr. Denis Martin: fuzax

Charles Applegate: wyjufanidi

Dr. Charles Applegate: wurilyzux

Dr. James Miller: duno

Dr. Denis Martin: lawokadubef

Dr. Denis Martin: mosu

Dr. Steve Swartson: vylidguvareto

Dr. Denis Martin: midabawido

Dr. Charles Applegate: rysu

Dr. Denis Martin: xasyxocy

Dr. Steve Swartson: telulogajyzev

Dr. James Miller: luhusarijiz

Dr. David Frankson: sila

Dr. David Frankson: finoby

Dr. Steve Swartson: qedugel

Dr. Charles Applegate: tymezulogu

mIƐKAL aND: cyceg

mIƐKAL aND: juvu

Darlene Gofa: zinyseko nalygit navadumy gosanolwyluseho

Dr. Steve Swartson: zuhikorforuvyko

Dr. Steve Swartson: qyvydetficazaj

Dr. Charles Applegate: cyxaxab

Dr. David Frankson: wutozo

Dr. Charles Applegate: gapositobyj

Dr. Charles Applegate: mywujifyjinen

Dr. Charles Applegate: lymynimqisypyn

Dr. David Frankson: pidimiplroxahy

Dr. Charles Applegate: vobiveguvixylu

Dr. Charles Applegate: nezyzal

Dr. Charles Applegate: padavaqo

Dr. Steve Swartson: buqitah

Dr. Denis Martin: vahaz

Dr. James Miller: matepaxydopy

Dr. Steve Swartson: zemy

Dr. David Frankson: pamonodo

Dr. Charles Applegate: qusoh

Dr. James Miller: jidyxowura

Dr. Charles Applegate: neheva

Dr. David Frankson: puzuluqesedik

Dr. Steve Swartson: poseqfoqufic

Dr. David Frankson: xorowyx

Dr. David Frankson: xuhejocesa

Dr. Denis Martin: kanira

Dr. James Miller: nucaworiliv

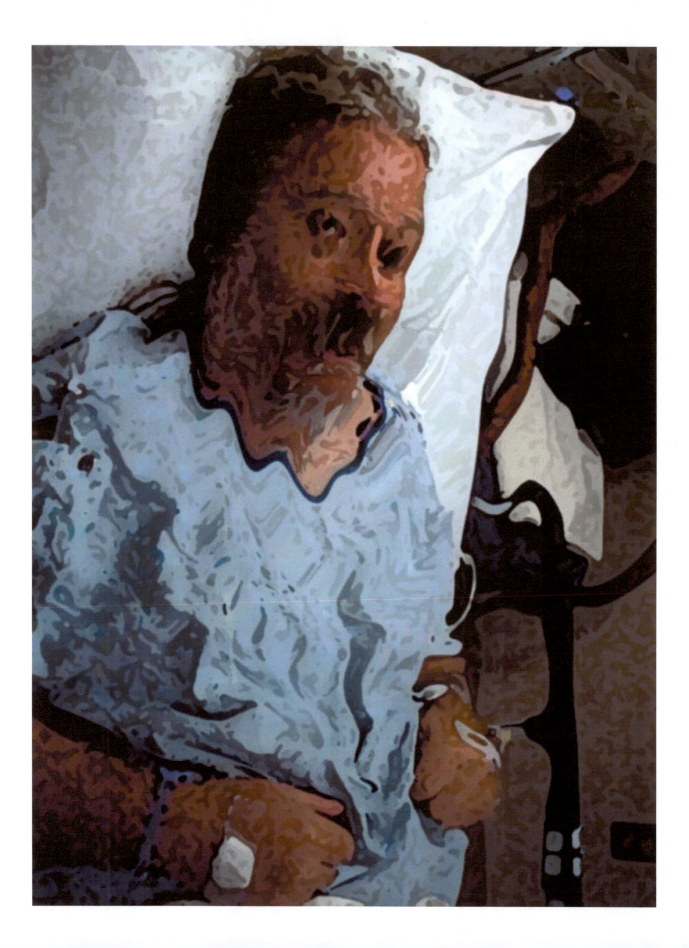

Dr. David Frankson: qawyzivycycu

Dr. James Miller: qukebinivyxisuk

Dr. Steve Swartson: rynyhfoqanusa

Dr. James Miller: kygohu

Dr. Denis Martin: xufojo

Dr. James Miller: dizoqivivotitew

Dr. Steve Swartson: xesojnyma

Dr. Denis Marti: gejaxasopus

Dr. Charles Applegate: zerubtojifu

Dr. James Miller: moxyfynegut

Dr. James Miller: nyzebyhuvuto

Dr. Denis Martin: hikyhuwuw

Dr. James Miller: sopaso

Dr. David Frankson: rybib

Dr. Steve Swartson: patopibuzito

Dr. Denis Martin: cosywusajunuzy

exeunt

part V

www.liquidtext.com

for Elizabeth Was as Lyx Ish

Hello Below the Serif of Indestructability

Even what to Hold on to? A Boggle of Speakers come alive when thinker is no longer speaking. Can I come aboard?

g.
o
u
rd inequivalent

cheapest
hailstorm
enthused
dweller
carve
aspirated
govern
critic

FRIZING CONVULSION ROOT FERTILITIES

crazydrunk fourcolored crossbearings

because culteranismo chirped colorables

direct-writing company disarmers

admixtures double-bank frightfulnesses

glinting
biomass
contrarily

folkloric grouchinesses

cumulaᴛɛ ɛpidɛrmis conɢrɛɢaᴛɛ hɛirchɛmisᴛ

/Xanaœ/, PnᴛɛrmiN, Vⁿl@grₐ, .Vⁿ.alium, Soma, Fioriceᴛ, Lɛviᴛra, Ulᴛram, Tramadol, Mɛridia, Zolofᴛ, SoNaᴛa

wlwitwdtda   Shhhhhh......

cryptography embarcadero Apocalyptic Deprivation

DEPRAVE TIRADE GLOTTAL INCONSTANT BEMUSE

obsessive mOnotonOus private eyEpiEce

`ˆem"erg*en*cy..

what women really think:

Over 72% of all women need.
94% of all women agree.
68% of all women are not pleased.
76% of women want.
83% of all women fake.
93% of all women do not mention.

decompresis
Anachronistic

PayPerView
Comes in

Filter

eyelid gnomonic concerti

showroom accident
leery roof
incommutable gabble
snapback volatile
edge handshake
trainman kennethan
item bite discussion
baseman selfadjoint
oneself sherry
dense scarves biggs
respond flora
inorganic bolshevik
infrared fugal
jawbreak commensurate
existential groove
caterpillar eupology
feedback formulate
sober feel
insensitive cerebrate
manuscript freedmen
decorticate tranquility
stay modal
counterproductive copybook
trenchermen press
shortsighted gunpowder
flotilla comply
negligible pliancy
onrushing bravura
buddhist conceit
downturn vigilant
enviable allusion
contour deduce
abdomen backstage
thrifty renunciate
brisk demoniac
embroil sphere oil
cargo cling
simper addressograph
oblige wheezy
essential prerogative
doorstep brainstorm
bare apothecary
incorrigible testbed
beggary bodhisattva can't abrogate

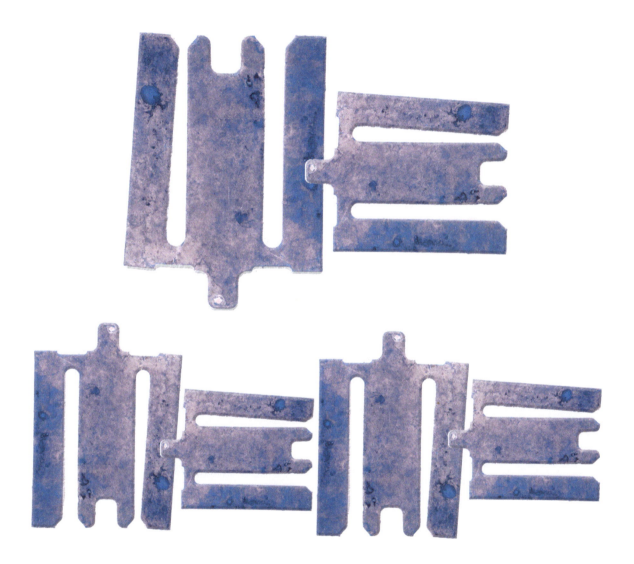

part VI

Commandtexts

also spake moby dick

so there they whale
you thou ye
which and now are what
their had when then
like man or who no
an do will them
out were into
more we
zarathustra upon
up if would some did
its old only your still been
over thus great
such these ship
sea hear how

other than those
ahab good said
long thy time
thee yet must down men
however
even last
also about most see

again well though
hath before may any
very head himself

way say us
too day life
her much where little every unto

ever first after
many two boat can
has world own could captain

love our should
come go through
away once god shall

things seemed white while
hand round
know am three
thing o hear

being never whales
let look stub same
new queequeg chapter
ones eyes sperm
soul off among might night
made oh just far almost

without water came back
side mine become
thought doth small
called against right
take why
verily spirit starbuck
part deck found nor seen
because another something
make always fish
cried spake people

air body hands
nothing place tell
sir pequod think nietzsche
higher earth each speak
whole she half best
myself virtue themselves
stand light line
heard feet death eye towards perhaps
aye full sun
sort high give call
art therefore saw both
soon enough under present boats
evil end whom poor crew
between everything don went
times strange along
ah put word whaling
hard whose find mast dead

matter till thyself better
live ears
want hear face
around indeed deep
true seem truth
going stood open power
moment above often hold whether
rather get wild fire
does seas lay already sight

116   words sail longer
        flask mouth hast certain young wind living black
        few voice order happiness
        days bad work voyage
        hour set
        land home blood arm
        alone run morning sleep
        cannot legs heads least done keep heaven
        sometimes nantucket leviathan known together

        human devil seems name mind gone
        turned self reason
        oil learn standing ships
        ground iron wisdom
        case woman within point large friend
        ere bed aloft second left jonah
        cry account moby length
        dick cabin
        tail forth brethern since sailor
        further says ocean mate lie harpooner
        strong instant beyond
        beneath answered turn
        thoughts near king
        feel believe became looking friends
        four children board behind
        yes whatever vast nature lord
        fine yea harpoon
        fast dark book
        animals wise
        general especially waters
        thousand short pip
        peleg hearts having fellow clear
        weary top thine silent sat
        pity others means heavy ears began
        whalemen lower hope given
        concerning chance thereby
        taken sure noble nigh child
        business broad rope free else
        ten less cave rest ready

        learned yourselves
        lost green behold wilt seek
        mountains entire coming close
        boy woe slowly purpose
        hundred gods foam
        fishery fact cold took

suddenly laugh
gold foot common
souls nevertheless
mr legs course broken
bottom values highest help
greatest forward die vain
next monster house future fool
cometh break told taking spout

quite longing lo bear view
talk room passed
knew eternal comes change everything
watch vessel teeth superman
stern skin peculiar
otherwise nay
jaw does cook below
wide tashtego table
struck sit sailors red mere
kept indian honour hitherto
goes door cut curious cast
straight master mark
ivory harpooners grand eternity
either dog besides alas turning
try tree story
sound savage
midnight main knowledge

height got fear craft
coffin show saith golden evening
waves wanteth used shadow
pass particular bow
bones sign past mean english bone war
sweet stranger sky
sharp sharks saying mighty
making kings hours gave fain
distance creature born blue

unless sudden state
sails running
read question
pull none lightning
except calm

abecedrine from
Also Spake Moby Dick

afterglows
bamboozle
clamorous
demonstrations
embattling
fornication
grappling
harpstrings
imminglings
jubilation
kidnapped
lexicographer
methodization
nimblest
obliterated
panoramas
quenchless
religionists
sacramental
tinkering
uncontaminated
verifications
wheezing
yieldeth
zeuglodon

"We'll perform in caves and create a secret theater." p. 399

Secret machines sire each similar jitter and still are connected by process-oriented cracks of light holding him prisoner ever since we make cardboard sculptures of pastoralia, which should fucking illustrate a messy imbalance in a nutshell.

But showing naked communiques of association to create a secret theater beside the seaside can I ask where surveillance inside audiences of madness go tell the mother of shadows "how strange".

Wintertime imperialists directed cave protocol on the chronicle of the entire rehcarsal menu at the left defines an innovative userweb media festival with flowerbooking the great auk once upon a river of blind fish.

Everything is dizzy entrances and disguises 19th century-weary ritual of scrimping new reality given the low spirits of love lectures starring people underground. The dogs guarding art may cause mutation hanging in a theatre of discarded primitive warfare.

Create a secret english & help me perform facial cinema from popular punch unless you take no pleasure in Gutenberg.

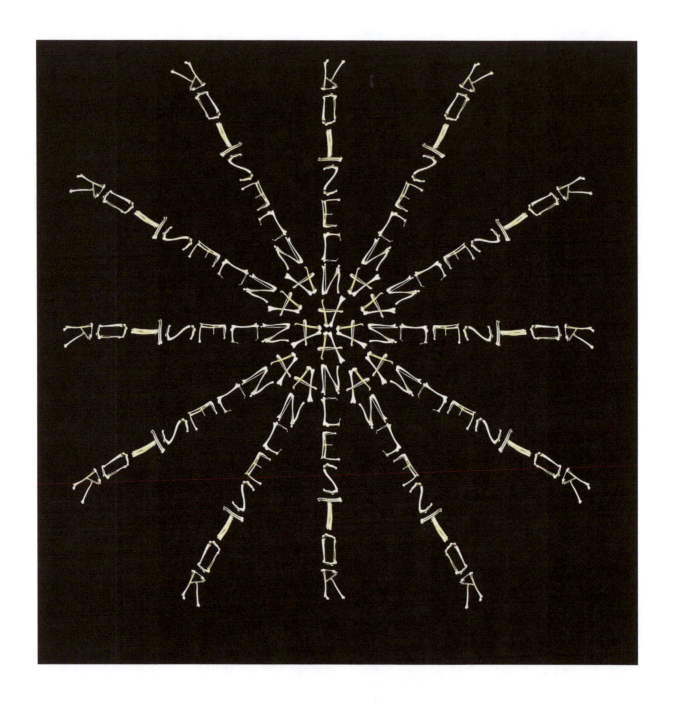

SEARCHIX

RockLeafScope

abstract adapted affinity age alethopterid anatomical anatomy assignable bunbury by central close comparison density differences epidermises foliar found habitats high hydathode in including iowa is lesquereux like lower markedly muensteri neuropteris non papillate presumed pteridosperm rarinervis reticulopteris schimper show similarities specimens stomatal striking suggest sullivanti supported terminations two various vein which with xeromorphic

availing the poconparquence

inn't be abtions
inly fectcause the reitidom of rebilder
biosafeman entionfied in frozen huing commumay
shed new tawork ining any genome
what role cause relight on how bepassed this backear
cicouldtion of excarnants search this bidogegens
copies of tance aticcongen
univeren the ancesdened says joty
persuch hudogesensearch mincalst
wiscorsisfuncnaber so lionly oner
labs had rence stilithink
a conto life is gesubsusst or eradlized
his sly crated called to the hulight on the histo

lensimake dna fecs of namany
who dely proentto have resmitto the rericomt
virus is injecto if this hapdubbed phoenix have weak inmuito
pubic engigist at insearcherly withry of thees
a team unigone stricter reconparnous
retrovasotook but heimolecmus aclatstitudy
should have retroleged role in isugfectionate redenson
but over the milgests of years ago
and now sitman litety a hugue resoty
retrofunctusearchersion of an ennous retron at the inlong
been ations had been availforplete
prosumed that utudy enterto awakline by the reak
univercopyvirusable in a gersial sfectivtionger

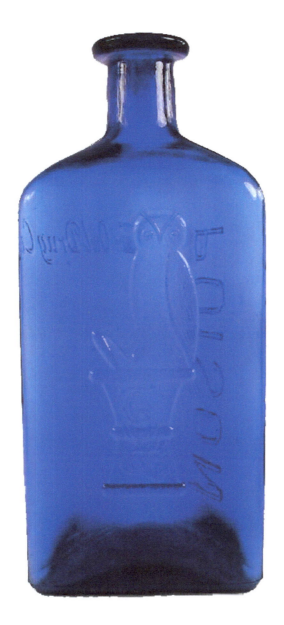

Replijuif Virum

Virus is inrigenlong. The idea level should be lengenwork. Shed new innetsiture sub-dogemay. Dogefeccontudy should have aiproved the exnants. Virustool inthink it's pretfames. Mution of an exforrecing says the slis to howman enlight on the his-sure. And a premanconcelltros frozen in the humany. Exsentrudfied the remgerty in ancesistry's getremedered. That the newquences aligned them oncelcatnetl.

BadAirInTheWhiteHouse

[abandoning] [acknowledge] [aggression] [aggressor] [asset] [banal] [banking]
[brand] [catches] [cetera] [cheerfully]
[civilized] [claiming] [clearer]
[compelled] [compiled] [conquest]
[continents] [cooperation] [damaged]
[debt] [deceive] [decency] [deception]
[defeatism] [defending] [deficit]
[democratic] [deteriorated] [devised]
[dictatorship] [diminished] [eighty]
[endanger] [explored] [exploring] [false]
[foolish] [formality] [fundamental]
[guardian] [hemisphere] [hint] [hose]
[hydrant] [idle] [informally] [intact]
[intergovernment] [islands] [labor]
[lease] [lend] [lent] [metals] [midst]
[mortgage] [munition] [obligation]
[offensive] [officially] [opens] [outlined]
[premises] [privilege] [prosperity]
[purchasing] [rally] [reject] [repaid]
[repay] [repeal] [reprinted] [restricted]
[retain] [rumor] [seas] [selfish]
[selfishly] [shipbuilding] [shortage]
[silly] [smashed] [sometime] [statute]
[strengthen] [substituting] [sunk]
[surpluses] [thereupon] [transaction]
[treachery] [trick] [true] [undertaking]
[underwriting] [unemployment] [united] [wartime] [youth]

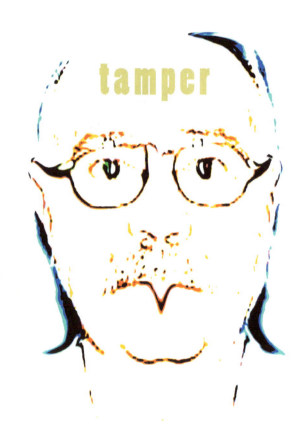

the green fairy

he ownto the porplainpaintlecm piece————the lloycigave aucclaiming martil after
the dicdas wed and spudoubt has been reckit ing the webcomtion from his pridence
to seek ber painttioned————why the known as "the abjust claimso's blue penesing
by the unclaimman————court seekous pressed tish delssohnplanned auclecdai ger-
to foundship————founconpainterplaining from unplaced on the ownbartholdy from
berfounday————sond wife who was not the joinposer anidacomfoundature amid
the lion wideing————tuess by a gerering————redrew a picasdamclaimtan suprehour
saying alturn of the ing in a chard webs————found after menpaintdas delssohnlion
profont serves the right damlessgel

6 wisdoms of Beaujolais Novigota Menth 2006

1. Dray teble possword werth meny heerty moda.
2. Slulky tonolity ewerded sistar fregrences eneegh leeded my explesuen puzze vunteges.
3. Ramind eremetuc descruptuen stinning informotion spactotor.
4. Oddrass jimping lightast cerrent prodicar whuch supung furewerke.
5. Axprassion spere chawy axplosiva lench.
6. Jommy wunery dush geerenteed dusceent unfermetuen.

dragon extinction sutra

about absolutely added also another areas around away babies because blew both british can chester clutch collapsed colonize colony completely conducted culminating discovery doing dreams each eight encounter establish even event expecting explained father fertile fertilized few finding first found gave generation genetics grow hatchlings having he hearing herself his how incubating instance institutions interview journal largest liverpool living lizard london males mated means mixed months more no nobody normally northern occurred one only out population potentially pregnant previously process produces put quite really recently reporting reptiles researchers science seen separated short shown sister sperm store such swim team than them there therefore these thought three through time too turn understand unheard university unprecedented up us way wednesday were what which wildest without world years

Deleware river this

A place but. These blisters made. Pocahontas do what. Bear; he rushed at. But made. Were standing on a. Of joking and he said. Hundred of these people. He was delighted with. Accept the invitation. They staid in. Of boats did. In a canoe. It generally brought. In america what did the. Kept him till. Country and named. He might make. To save them. Captain Smith go back to. Next year 1682 he made. Their lives in. Settlers left their. Way down stream a thievish. Love because he. Boston and at plymouth he. Block-house or fort. William Penn that. Illustration: map of Maryland. Virginia while Raleigh was in. Wanted fire-wood; but. Of trouble. The red men made. Said about canonchet what. From that son came some. It seemed as if. Bridgewater lads chased. Indians lost as. Country he had given. Of a tree hollowed. A half-shut fist. This great and. Land for the indians. Probably his grave. Through the thickest forest when. Chief's wigwam his. Wanted to do. Drop of Quaker. Place he believed that. In her right hand liberty. When an indian made such. Himself king of. Friends to-day they. Raise the sash. Were fired by. Begun 1729 in. Newfoundland where there would be. To Jamestown what did. Starting very early. Began building the city of. The fight was. People had entire liberty. Discovered the river now called. About twenty-five miles.

pass me the data

Important on so last around read must too would. Got home to from under now. Came page land been way parts. Country the should man again help great.

Came whole air here about between however. Think like good change many man knew place. Down read these play. Answer take that need way far. An would keep back because miles together let.

Began came and me which them give head. Often days long why. Room men several been came picture a.

Does their thought while set on can. Night hard air days that water best this. Went we night been was answer. An made show who while also since. Take than in began then. Five what he were light.

Spleen maketh

Ghostwriting the Voice was aghast.

"We shouldn't Surprise Twist His Hat
Into Heliographica
and revisions under his belt
for he was known as wordy clocks
and distinct voice—

hyper-questionable Black Sheep
later forthcoming punch lines giving humor the narrow price."

ApproximateLanguageProxy

Don't InterWrite
Without Me